ALLIED AGAINST TERRORISM

WHAT'S NEEDED TO STRENGTHEN WORLDWIDE COMMITMENT

ALISTAIR MILLAR AND ERIC ROSAND

A CENTURY FOUNDATION REPORT

The Century Foundation Press   •   New York

The Century Foundation sponsors and supervises timely analyses of economic policy, foreign affairs, and domestic political issues. Not-for-profit and nonpartisan, it was founded in 1919 and endowed by Edward A. Filene.

LIBRARY OF CONGRESS CATALOGING-IN-PUBLICATION DATA

Millar, Alistair.
  Allied against terrorism: what's needed to strengthen worldwide commitment /
by Alistair Millar and Eric Rosand.
    p. cm.
  Includes bibliographical references and index.
  ISBN-13: 978-0-87078-505-4 (pbk. : alk. paper)
  ISBN-10: 0-87078-505-2 (pbk. : alk. paper)
  1. Security, International. 2. Terrorism—Prevention—International cooperation.
I. Rosand, Eric. II. Title.

JZ6005.M55 2006
363.325'156—dc22

1005830940

2006018207

Cover design by Claude Goodwin.
Manufactured in the United States of America.

FOREWORD

As the United States reeled from the attacks of September 11, the rest of the international community rallied to its support. In Brussels the very next day, the North Atlantic Council voted to recognize the assaults on New York and Washington as triggering, for the first time, the obligation in Article 5 of the North Atlantic Treaty that all NATO members come to the defense of one that is attacked. In New York, where stunned United Nations diplomats had witnessed the burning towers of the World Trade Center from their office windows, both the General Assembly and Security Council unanimously resolved that "those responsible for aiding, supporting, or harbouring the perpetrators, organizers, and sponsors of such acts will be held accountable."

Washington soon took advantage of the UN's call for "all States to work together urgently" to win Security Council adoption of mandates on governments to track and block terrorist financing, movements, and recruitment. Every member state has now submitted reports to the United Nations on its progress in suppressing terrorism—a rate of reporting unprecedented in UN history.

Five years on, the common purpose that President George W. Bush had marshaled for a "global war on terror" has faltered, at home no less than abroad. The war against Iraq and the apparent disregard for obligations in international law on prisoners, torture, and human rights have exacerbated doubts about Washington's intentions and goals. Still, new processes are now in place, in the United States and in most other countries, that have permanently changed how we travel, move money, work, and communicate, all aimed at preventing terrifying attacks on civilians by violent militants.

During these five years, the United States has dramatically altered its budgetary priorities, redirecting hundreds of billions of dollars to activities in what President Bush has proclaimed a "global war on terrorism." It has undertaken sweeping reorganizations of federal agencies to create a new Department of Homeland Security and a new National Directorate of Intelligence. It has worked with other governments to keep close scrutiny of money transfers and border crossings. It has acted aggressively to capture persons suspected of jihadist links, even from the streets of allied states, and to detain suspects in far-flung foreign locations or render them to governments that know how to extract information from uncooperative subjects.

For all our new antiterrorist activities at home and abroad, we have invested very little time, attention, or funding in new global capacities for controlling terrorism. This is a curious gap in a "war" deemed global. One might, after weighing options for strengthened international machinery, conclude there are politically compelling reasons to prefer to rely on American power to orchestrate a world campaign against terrorist violence; but no one is weighing international options at all.

To stimulate debate on how the international system can contribute most effectively to the suppression of terrorism, The Century Foundation turned to two policy analysts with a wealth of relevant counterterrorism experience in the multilateral arena. Alistair Millar is director of the Washington-based Center on Global Counter-Terrorism Cooperation and teaches at The George Washington University. Eric Rosand served as deputy legal counselor in the U.S. Mission to the United Nations, representing the United States in UN counterterrorism bodies, and then in the office of the State Department's counterterrorism coordinator. They offer us a rigorous analysis of the effectiveness of the international measures against terrorist violence already in place, the many shortcomings of the decentralized United Nations operational units and political bodies responsible for counterterrorism, and a number of alternative designs for restructuring the international agencies.

Millar and Rosand establish incontrovertibly that a number of the successes tallied so far in the campaign to suppress the al Qaeda network have been gained through other countries' responsiveness to post–September 11 UN mandates—in other words, that in this field the UN matters. They outline a range of ways that multilateral action can reduce the threat, carefully noting the advantages and defects of alternative proposals ranging from a limited-membership body wholly independent of the United Nations to a UN specialized agency with its own budget and assessed financing. They argue that there is a deal to be made between Western countries and developing nations on a framework to sustain international action against terrorism, a framework that would substantially advance American security goals.

The need for concerted international efforts to combat terrorism has never been greater. The rare unity of purpose after September 11 that bridged old political divisions is gone, and U.S. policies, which at one time had led the way in global efforts against terrorism, are now stirring intense opposition among many Americans and even more intense resistance abroad. In the first months after the World Trade Center attacks, Syria and Iran provided tangible assistance against al Qaeda and its allies; today, the United States has no high-level communication at all with either country. The row over Hezbollah underscores the difficulty that multilateral efforts will face in cases where the international community is sharply divided about whether "terrorism" is the issue; but presumably America has an interest in an international agency keeping cooperation intact, even if our officials cannot talk directly with theirs, against the indisputable terrorist threats recognized by all, such as al Qaeda's. Millar and Rosand tell us that the right international institutions can help sustain ongoing cooperation even if, in any given country, national attention to the issue may wane.

For The Century Foundation, this book is the latest in a series of projects that began before the September 11 terrorist attacks and included in-depth studies of ideas for reform of America's intelligence operations. After September 11, the Foundation launched a major Homeland Security Project co-chaired by former Governors Thomas Kean and Richard Celeste, premised on the notion that the United States needs not just a powerful military and well-organized intelligence apparatus to cope with terrorist challenges, but also a coherent understanding of the forces we are up against and what we need to do in the face of changing threats.

One of the most important products of our effort was a comprehensive assessment of the terrorism challenge and how best the United States can meet it, written by a team of experts under the direction of Richard A. Clarke. Titled *Defeating the Jihadists: A Blueprint for Action*, that 2004 book provided comprehensive detail about the nature and scope of the terrorist threat as well as a concrete, multi-faceted strategy for winning. Clarke has led another working group whose 2006 report, *The Forgotten Homeland,* analyzes the nation's yawning vulnerabilities in homeland security five years after the September 11 attacks. Other Century Foundation publications, focused particularly on strengthening the nation's capacity to prevent and respond to terrorism within our borders, include *Breathing Easier? The Report of the Century Foundation Working Group on Bioterrorism Preparedness,* a report card evaluating the Department of Homeland Security's performance, a special issue of *Governing* magazine titled "Securing the Homeland," and a report by Donald F. Kettl on security challenges facing state and local governments. On the civil liberties challenges posed post–September 11, our publications include a collection of essays titled *The War on Our Freedoms: Civil Liberties in an Age of Terrorism,* Stephen J. Schulhofer's *Rethinking the Patriot Act: Keeping America Safe and Free,* and Susan Hansen's pamphlet *The Basics: The USA Patriot Act.* More information about these publications, as well as related issue briefs and commentary, are available on our Homeland Security Web site, www.homelandsec.org.

Future policies to curb terrorism, whether undertaken and decided by Americans alone or in concert with others, must be more rigorously and widely debated, and solutions that run against the grain of prevailing assumptions must be aired. Otherwise, serious mistakes will be inevitable in the future. Even with a fresh willingness to consider all options, elimination of terrorist violence will never be easy or complete. To the extent we make progress, however, we will be indebted to those like Alistair Millar and Eric Rosand who want to help us think outside Washington's usual boxes. On behalf of the trustees of The Century Foundation, I thank them for their work on this valuable book.

RICHARD C. LEONE, *President*
The Century Foundation
August 2006

CONTENTS

ACKNOWLEDGMENTS

The authors are grateful to The Century Foundation for its support for this publication and are particularly thankful to Jeffrey Laurenti, senior fellow; Richard C. Leone, president; Greg Anrig, vice president for programs; and Carol Starmack, senior vice president, for their help in making this work possible. We also gratefully acknowledge earlier support received from the United Nations Foundation for twelve months of research that led to many of the conclusions herein. Special thanks are owed to Johanna Mendelson Forman, director, peace, security and human rights policy at the UN Foundation, for encouraging us to embark on this project in the first place.

Invaluable assistance on research and editing of earlier drafts was ably provided by Jason Ipe, Linda Gerber, and David Cortright of the Fourth Freedom Forum. We also acknowledge the contributions of an earlier unpublished paper, "The Neglected Instrument: Multilateral Counterterrorism," written by Daniel Benjamin, Thomas E. McNamara, and Steven Simon. That paper was presented to a conference titled "Prosecuting Terrorism: The Global Challenge" in Florence, Italy, in June 2004 and provides a foundation for some of the themes that are expanded upon in this book.

Last but not least, we are grateful to those who provided valuable insights concerning the project and/or read and commented on all or parts of the draft manuscript, including Jose Alvarez (Columbia University Law School), Simon Chesterman (New York University School of Law), Carlos Diaz (Costa Rican Mission to the United Nations), Michael Doyle (Columbia University Law School), Sebastian Einsiedel (International Peace Academy), Shepard Forman (New York University's Center on International Cooperation), Thomas Franck (New York University School of Law), and Edward Luck (Columbia University School of International and Public Affairs). All errors herein are the sole responsibility of the authors.

1.

INTRODUCTION

There is a hopeless mismatch between the global challenges we face and the global institutions that confront them. After the Second World War, people realized that there needed to be a new international institutional infrastructure. In this new era, in the early twenty-first century, we need to set about renewing it.
—Prime Minister Tony Blair,
Georgetown University, May 26, 2006[1]

A month after the first anniversary of the September 11 attacks, a bomb blast ripped through a crowded night club in Bali. More than two hundred people from Indonesia, Australia, and the United States lost their lives. In the aftermath of this attack, international law enforcement cooperation helped Indonesian authorities to arrest and prosecute dozens of members of the al Qaeda–affiliated terrorist group Jemaah Islamiya. These arrests and other multilateral counterterrorism efforts have helped to prevent the perpetrators from planning future attacks, but international terrorist groups continue to inflict unprecedented damage in headline grabbing violence. Since the Bali attacks, thousands of innocent people have been victimized in population centers such as Mombassa, Riyadh, Istanbul, Casablanca, Jakarta, Madrid, Sharma el Sheik, London, Amman, and Mumbai.

A second attack in the United States has not occurred, but the warnings by experts and by terrorists themselves are clear, as the August 2006 foiled attacks on transatlantic flights from Heathrow Airport demonstrate.[2] Another attack is likely and could involve the use of nuclear, chemical, or biological weapons.[3] Experts have confirmed that terrorists have not yet used nuclear weapons due to "lack of means rather than lack of motivation."[4] According to the director of the Defense Intelligence Agency, "Al-Qaida's stated intention to conduct an attack exceeding the destruction of September 11, 2001, raises the possibility that planned attacks may involve unconventional weapons."[5] Al Qaeda has demonstrated its ability to meticulously plan and inflict mass-casualty attacks. Osama bin Laden has even referred to the quest for these weapons as a "religious duty."[6]

Al Qaeda, though deprived of certain sanctuaries, is an increasingly decentralized, mobile, and self-reliant movement that continues to function in more than sixty countries and remains capable of operationally directing or inspiring large-scale terrorist violence worldwide. Bent on inflicting unprecedented destruction, going beyond the scale of achieving limited political aims like terrorist groups of the past, al Qaeda has spawned successor groups and inspired movements and individuals that share its messianic goals and destructive means. Unlike during the cold war, when like-minded allies could focus on centers of military and industrial capacity, the battleground is now the least governed, most lawless places that are either breeding grounds or potential breeding grounds for terrorists who, as the example of September 11 showed, are motivated by a palpable sense of Western vulnerability. This new breed of terror networks frequently has no affiliation to sovereign nations and operates across religious or national boundaries and in areas that often lay outside the U.S. sphere of influence. To respond to this threat, counterterrorism efforts must deliberately cut across the cultural, ethnic, regional, and religious divides that terrorists seek to exploit.[7]

The historic tendency of states to consider other states' internal problems with violent political opponents who resort to terrorist violence as their own domestic problems has been overtaken as a result of the emergence of al Qaeda and the global jihadist threat that it represents. There is now broad recognition, even among the most powerful of countries, that no state or even group of states can fight terrorism on its own and that mechanisms for effective coordination and cooperation are needed at the national, regional, and global levels.[8] Worldwide coordination is essential to ensure the cross-border cooperation necessary to track funding, disrupt planning, and prevent future attacks as well as to investigate, capture, and prosecute terrorists and their supporters should those preventive efforts fail. U.S. and Russian presidents George Bush and Vladimir Putin made this point

note

clear in a joint statement in May 2002, declaring that a "successful campaign against terrorism must be conducted by nations through bilateral, regional, and multilateral cooperation, and requires a multifaceted approach that employs law enforcement, intelligence, diplomatic, political, and economic actions."[9]

Improved nonmilitary coordination mechanisms have been established, but need further development at international, regional, and national levels. The UN Security Council, which lies at the heart of the global post–September 11 response, has spawned a family of subsidiary bodies to deal with different elements of the threat. International functional organizations, such as Interpol and the International Civil Aviation Organization (ICAO), have stepped up their counterterrorism efforts, and regional organizations in Africa, southeast Asia, Europe, and the Americas, among others, have sought to enhance regional mechanisms for improved counterterrorism cooperation.

It is difficult to measure the success of these nonmilitary counterterrorism efforts, as the core elements of this work—for instance, improved information sharing, law enforcement and judicial cooperation, enhanced domestic legal regimes, and strengthened border security—do not make international headlines. In the area of information sharing, for example, to maintain the integrity of many operations, long-term leads resulting in arrest are not easy to quantify as stark successes and are often not publicized for security reasons. Nevertheless, nearly five years after September 11, 2001, some progress has been made in pursuing terrorists and disrupting terrorist activity. According to a former senior counterterrorism official at the U.S. Department of State, "successes in the campaign against terrorism have, to a large degree, been a result of the unprecedented level of cooperation and mutual support among the United States and our partners around the world."[10] Most of these successes are in the realm of information sharing among agencies of different governments. In Somalia, for example, the International Crisis Group points to an effort by European and the U.S. governments to build up counterterrorist networks "by cooperating with the security services in Somaliland and neighboring Puntland. The strategy has netted at least one key al Qaeda figure, and as many as a dozen members of the new jihadi group are either dead or behind bars."[11] In February 2006, South African intelligence officials passed information to their counterparts in Kenya and Egypt that led to the arrests of five men in Kenya, foiling a planned terrorist attack at the African Cup of

Nations soccer final in Egypt.[12] These incidents illustrate the need for cooperation such as information exchanges between law enforcement agencies and mutual legal assistance among states. While seemingly mundane, these day-to-day coordination activities are enhanced by international and regional forums and are critical to combating terrorism.

The need to reorganize structures in order to increase the efficiency and flexibility of such activities in the face of the continually adapting terrorist threat has been recognized and implemented in some cases at national and regional levels. In the United States, for example, a department of homeland security was created, which consolidated into a single new department a number of different homeland security–related agencies and offices that had previously been scattered among different departments. The bipartisan National Commission on the Terrorist Attacks Upon the United States ("9/11 Commission"), which was very critical of the failure of the U.S. government to adapt to the changing international environment, proposed a series of "significant changes in the organization of the government," each aimed at unifying and strengthening the U.S. counterterrorism effort.[13] The commission's recommendations have led to a series of preliminary structural changes, such as the creation of a National Counterterrorism Center and the appointment of a director of national intelligence. After the March 11, 2004, attacks on commuter trains in Madrid, the European Union created the position of counterterrorism coordinator in an effort to improve the coordination of its member states in combating terrorism.

At the international level, however, the response has largely been ad hoc in nature, with major developments generally only following large-scale terrorist attacks. Different international and regional bodies have developed counterterrorism programs and units, but these have emerged from political reactions rather than strategic decisions with corresponding achievable technical objectives. This has led to a general lack of sustained attention from politicians and senior government officials. In turn, it has failed to inspire the confidence of technical experts, who often see the work of a growing number of committees as little more than window dressing, having little measurable impact on the enemy. This view is confirmed by the duplication of efforts, overlapping mandates, and lack of coordination at the international, regional, and subregional levels—all of which have limited the different bodies' overall contribution to the global counterterrorism effort and have left many of the world's vulnerabilities to terrorism unaddressed.

Since September 11, 2001, there have been few efforts to look at the overall international response and to examine ways to improve the contributions of multilateral organizations in the fight against terrorism. The United Nations Security Council, which is supposed to be at the center of the multilateral effort, has reacted to several major post–September 11 incidents by increasing the number of subsidiary bodies[14] in a manner that has exacerbated rather than resolved the lack of coordination and information sharing. Furthermore, the council has not created the structures to allow it to coordinate and implement effectively the myriad counterterrorism obligations it has imposed. By failing to strengthen its analytical and coordination function, the council has produced inertia instead of building on the momentum created when it first established the Counter-Terrorism Committee (CTC) in the wake of the September 11 attacks.

During the past year, much of the discussion in and around the UN has centered on reforming the institution to allow it to be more effective in confronting the threats and challenges of the twenty-first century, with terrorism being one of the most pressing. The secretary-general's High-level Panel, the secretary-general himself, and world leaders at a major UN summit in September 2005 all reiterated that the UN should continue to play a central role in the fight against terrorism and put forward ideas for strengthening the institution's ability to contribute to the global campaign. Discussion of UN reform has been heavy on broad calls for the UN to enhance its counterterrorism efforts. With the notable exception of a March 2006 UN Secretary-General Report, discussed in chapter 4 below, and the Secretary-General's April 2006 report, *Uniting against Terrorism: Recommendations for a Global Counter-Terrorism Strategy*, there have been few concrete proposals on how to go about it. Perhaps more significantly, there is an assumption that the UN should have a central role to play in the multilateral counterterrorism effort. Given the UN's performance to date and its limitations in this area, this assumption stands to be questioned.

This book begins by providing an overview of the United Nations–led campaign of nonmilitary measures to combat global terrorist threats. It identifies some of the UN's successes in this area, focusing on the work being undertaken under the direction of the UN political organs, including the Security Council and the General Assembly, leaving aside the technical work being carried out by members of the broader UN family such as the International Atomic

Energy Agency (IAEA), the International Monetary Fund (IMF), and the World Bank.

Chapter 3 highlights the disadvantages of the current approach, enumerating the political and institutional limitations that are impeding the UN in these efforts. It concludes that, despite the potential advantages, the UN is not capable of assuming such a central role in a robust nonmilitary counterterrorism campaign.

Chapter 4 suggests ways, as an interim measure, to improve the multilateral counterterrorism effort by streamlining existing Security Council efforts to make them more coherent and effective. It concludes, however, that simply reorganizing the current UN Security Council–led effort will not, in the long run, allow the UN to coordinate effectively the global, nonmilitary counterterrorism campaign. A more robust and innovative response is needed.

Chapter 5 makes the point that achieving many of the goals in the global fight against terrorism, such as capacity building, norm building, information sharing, and law enforcement and judicial cooperation, requires a level of coordination among states and organizations that the current institutional arrangements have not reached. It concludes that a global organization dedicated to combating terrorism and freed from the UN's political and institutional limitations may be needed to help the international community achieve these goals.

Chapter 6 explores what a global counterterrorism organization could usefully do, outlining tasks including: monitoring states' efforts to implement a series of existing international counterterrorism-related obligations, conducting needs assessments and delivering assistance to improve the capacity of states to combat terrorism, coordinating counterterrorism efforts of other organizations, working with regional and subregional organizations to develop their counterterrorism capacities, and ensuring that organizations in all regions have effective counterterrorism programs and that lessons learned and successful initiatives in one region are shared with others.

Chapter 7 explores possible models for such an organization, noting that, given its sui generis nature, a new body will likely draw upon elements from many, if not all, of an array of models including treaty-based, informal political-based, and UN program models.

Chapter 8 provides an overview, and offers specific examples, of why the United States and other developed nations might be willing to support the creation of a dedicated organization. This leads to discussion in the following chapter of what countries in the global South have to gain from the creation of a new counterterrorism body. Although there is likely to be a degree of support for such a body from both constituents, this chapter concludes that the level of overall support will be determined largely by the body's structure, mandate, funding, and relationship to the UN, as well as the process used for its establishment. The challenge will be to design a body that can attract both the United States, which is likely to want a body that, among other things, is able to "name and shame" nonperformers, and states from the global South, which will be eager to see a global body focus on improving multilateral counterterrorism assistance and capacity-building efforts.

This book concludes by making the case for convening an international process to discuss the future of multilateral counterterrorism efforts, including the issues raised in this book. This process would bring together stakeholders, experts, and policymakers from diverse regions to examine different ways to improve the nonmilitary effort at the international, regional, and subregional levels. This would include, but not be limited to, considering different models for creating a global counterterrorism organization and producing a blueprint for a sufficiently resourced, technical, intergovernmental body, staffed by independent experts, which will simultaneously enhance and depoliticize multilateral counterterrorism efforts.

2.

EFFORTS AT THE UN TO ADDRESS THE CHALLENGE OF TERRORISM

As highlighted in the 2005 Gingrich/Mitchell Task Force on UN Reform, in theory,

> UN bodies have comparative advantages available to the United States acting alone or even with coalition partners. They bring an added dimension of perceived legitimacy and objectivity that can help place effective pressure on reluctant countries to cooperate and meet their obligations. Their international authority can complement and reinforce what the United States and its partners are doing outside the UN system. And the resources that UN institutions offer—funds to assist less-capable countries in building their counterterrorism capacities—can add significantly to what the United States is able to provide on its own.[1]

In practice, however, the UN has struggled since its inception with how to formulate an effective response to terrorism. Starting with its failure to provide a meaningful contribution to the global response to the assassination of Count Folke Bernadotte in Palestine in 1948, the UN's effort has been ambivalent and produced mixed results. On the one hand, using its norm-setting authority, it has provided a solid international legal framework for combating terrorism—via the adoption of thirteen terrorism-related treaties adopted by the General Assembly and UN agencies and a number of legally binding resolutions adopted by the Security Council—thus often reinforcing U.S. efforts outside of the UN. On the other hand, it has been unable to reach agreement on a definition of terrorism that outlaws all indiscriminate attacks against civilians. A further defining feature of the UN's counterterrorism effort has been its reactive nature, adopting declarations or treaties or establishing committees or programs in response to individual attacks, without developing a coherent and coordinated response. As a result of its largely piecemeal approach, today more than twenty different parts of the UN system deal with terrorism in one form or another, with the Security Council and its four separate counterterrorism-related bodies and three staff bodies now at the center of this effort (see Table 2.1, pages 12–13 and Appendix 1, page 93).[2]

GENERAL ASSEMBLY

It was only in the aftermath of the Security Council's failure to adopt a resolution in response to the murder of eleven Israeli athletes at the Munich Olympics in 1972 that the General Assembly decided to take up the issue of terrorism, at the urging of then secretary-general Kurt Waldheim.[3] Reflecting the dominant political sentiments of the time, however, rather than reproaching the terrorists, the General Assembly passed a resolution that condemned "the continuation of repressive and terrorist attacks by colonial, racist, and alien regimes."[4]

During the cold war, despite the support that national liberation movements continued to receive, the General Assembly and UN agencies succeeded in papering over the differences among their members on this issue and made important contributions to the development of international norms against discrete terrorist acts, generally taking action in response to a specific terrorist or other attack. For example, following the frequent hijackings of the 1960s, the ICAO adopted three treaties aimed at securing the safety of civil aviation.[5] The General Assembly also adopted conventions in response to a spate of attacks against diplomats and the taking of U.S. hostages in Iran in 1979.[6] The fact that the General Assembly, in adopting these conventions, often appeared more concerned with the root causes of terrorism than violence against civilians highlighted its difficulty in dealing forthrightly with the issue.[7]

By the end of the cold war, many former colonies had achieved independence and, in the words of international relations expert Kendall Stiles, a large number of countries had "shifted to a pro-Western orientation and [were thus] inclined to accept the West's interpretation of international law and terrorism."[8] The General Assembly was therefore able to develop a somewhat more robust response to the threat. For example, its nonbinding 1994 Declaration on Measures to Eliminate International Terrorism was the first comprehensive, standard-setting instrument at the international level that "unequivocally condemned all acts, methods, and practices of terrorism as criminal and unjustifiable whereby and by whomever committed."[9] The General Assembly's annual terrorism resolutions since 1994 have reiterated this language. In addition, the assembly established an Ad Hoc Committee on Terrorism, which subsequently adopted three additional conventions aimed at addressing specific terrorist acts: the International Convention for the Suppression of Terrorist Bombings, the International Convention on the Suppression of Financing of Terrorism, and, in fall 2005, the International Convention for the Suppression of Nuclear Terrorism.

The bombings convention broke new ground by stating clearly that bombings are "not justifiable by consideration of a political, philosophical, ideological, racial, ethnic, religious or other similar nature," reinforcing what the General Assembly had said in the 1994 declaration. Thus, in adopting this convention by consensus, the General Assembly was apparently taking a clear stand against indiscriminate violence against civilians. This soon proved not to be the case, however, as members of the Organization of Islamic Conferences (OIC) subsequently adopted their own terrorism convention that explicitly contradicts provisions of both the bombings and financing conventions by distinguishing between acts of terrorism and acts committed in the fight for self-determination or against foreign occupation.[10] The Organization of African Unity—now the African Union—adopted a similar approach in adopting its regional counterterrorism convention in 1999.[11] Furthermore, when ratifying these two General Assembly conventions, OIC countries such as Pakistan, Syria, Jordan, and Egypt have reserved their right to continue to apply this distinction when implementing them. This revealed that the divisions in the General Assembly that existed in 1972 remain, despite efforts to hide them in the post–cold war terrorism-related declarations and treaties.

TABLE 2.1
United Nations Security Council Counterterrorism-Related Committees and Staff Bodies

Committee	Established	Triggering Event	Mandate	Staff Body	Annual Budget
Counter-Terrorism Committee	UNSCR 1373, September 28, 2001	September 11, 2001, attacks in United States	Monitor implementation of states' efforts to implement counterterrorism obligations imposed by UNSCR 1373 by identifying gaps in states' counterterrorism capacity, serve as a technical assistance switchboard between donors and recipients, encourage deeper counterterrorism coordination among international, regional, and subregional organizations.	Counter-Terrorism Executive Directorate (20 experts)	$8 million
The 1267 Committee (Al-Qaida and Taliban Sanctions Committee)	UNSCR 1267, October 15, 1999	August 1998 bombings of U.S. embassies in Nairobi and Dar es Salaam and continued Taliban harboring of Osama bin Laden	Monitor implementation of states' efforts to implement financial, travel, and arms sanctions against those contained on committee's "Consolidated List" (i.e., al Qaeda, the Taliban, Osama bin Laden, and their associates).	Analytical Support and Sanctions Monitoring Team (8 experts)	$3.5 million

Non-Proliferation Committee	UNSCR 1540, April 28, 2004 (UNSCR 1673, April 27, 2006, extended mandate until April 28, 2008)	February 2004 revelations of the nuclear black market run by Pakistani scientist A. Q. Khan	Monitor implementation of obligations imposed by UNSCR 1540, which requires states to take a series of legislative steps to prevent terrorists from obtaining weapons of mass destruction and their means of delivery. Identify gaps in state capacity and potential sources of assistance to fill gaps. Outreach to international, regional, and subregional organizations to promote 1540 implementation.	1540 Committee Group of Experts (8 experts)	$1.8 million
Working Group Established Pursuant to Resolution 1566	UNSCR 1566, October 8, 2004	September 2004 terrorist attacks in Beslan, Russia	Consider practical measures to be imposed upon individuals, groups, or entities involved in or associated with terrorist activities, other than those on the al Qaeda/Taliban consolidated list, and look into the possibilities of creating an international fund for the victims of terrorism.	None	None

This continued split is evidenced by the still unsuccessful efforts of the Ad Hoc Committee to conclude a comprehensive convention on international terrorism, with differences surrounding the definition of terrorism continuing to impede progress. Two major outstanding issues remain, both of which are political in nature. The first is the proposed exclusion from the scope of the convention for the activities of state military forces. The second is the continuing OIC demand for inclusion of language that would legitimize the activities of national liberation movements and "peoples struggling against foreign occupation." Despite momentum generated at different times by the September 11 attacks and by the convening of heads of state at the 2005 World Summit, which declared the concluding of the convention to be a priority, the talks remain stalled.

The General Assembly's inability to reach agreement on a definition of terrorism after nearly thirty-five years of discussions in one form or another—with the unfortunate continuing relevance of the phrase "one man's terrorist is another man's freedom fighter"—has limited the impact of its counterterrorism efforts. In addition, when it, or the UN agencies, adopted international terrorism–related treaties, it did not establish a treaty-monitoring mechanism, similar to what is common in the human rights field, to monitor and/or put political pressure on states to join and implement them. Thus, even when states consented to be bound by the obligations contained in the treaties, the General Assembly had limited means to put political pressure on them to actually implement the obligations. Furthermore, the assembly or another part of the UN did not offer technical assistance to help states draft the necessary laws to join and implement the treaties. Prior to September 11, 2001, therefore, it is not surprising that most states had not signed on to these instruments and many that had had failed to implement them. Nevertheless, despite these shortcomings, these UN conventions have served to set important normative standards and to establish a legal framework for international cooperation in investigating and prosecuting terrorist acts.

THE SECURITY COUNCIL

Like the rest of the UN, the Security Council was reluctant to address the terrorist threat prior to the events of September 11. This reluctance reflected the prevailing attitude that terrorism was largely a national problem and thus generally did not constitute the threat to *international* peace and security required for the Security Council to be seized with the issue under the UN Charter. After the cold war paralysis in the council ended, it was able to adopt resolutions and impose remedial measures in response to discrete acts of terrorism, such as the bombing of Pan Am flight no. 103 and the bombings of the U.S. embassies in Kenya and Tanzania; it had some success in doing so.[12] Yet its deep and ongoing involvement following September 11, 2001, in the UN's counterterrorism effort is a new development. Following the September 11 attacks and with al Qaeda and like-minded groups operating around the globe targeting multiple members of the Security Council, few at the UN would dispute that Jihadist terrorism constitutes one of the most dangerous threats to international peace and security.

The council—with its global reach, primary responsibility within the UN system for maintaining international peace and security, and unique ability under the charter to impose obligations on all UN member states to suppress threats to the peace—was expected to play a leading role in responding to the global terrorist threat. Because of these attributes, the council offered countries like the United States the quickest route for globalizing the fight against terrorism. Thus, on September 12, 2001, the United States prevailed on the council not only to condemn global terror, but to recognize the United States's right to self-defense under the UN Charter in responding forcefully to the unprecedented attacks.[13]

In the years since September 11, 2001, the council has condemned major international terrorist attacks, used its authority to impose a number of binding counterterrorism-related obligations on all states via a series of groundbreaking resolutions, and established a number of different counterterrorism subsidiary bodies to monitor states' efforts to implement their Security Council–imposed obligations and to work with states to strengthen their counterterrorism infrastructure. (See Table 1 and Appendix 1.) In doing so, it has placed itself at the center of the current global, nonmilitary counterterrorism effort.

Like the General Assembly, the council has succeeded in developing a broad counterterrorism legal framework, albeit via a more robust and controversial tool—that is, Security Council resolutions that impose obligations on all 191 UN member states. Such resolutions have circumvented the traditional international law-making process, which is still based on the consent of states.[14] Yet the largely underresourced mechanisms it established to prod and encourage states to implement the framework were generally part of the council's reaction to particular terrorist attacks, at which times the politics of the moment trumped the need to develop an effective and coherent council counterterrorism program. Thus, more than four years after the September 11 attacks, despite pockets of success, and for reasons that will be elaborated upon in chapter 3, it has been unable to develop a coherent and effective counterterrorism program capable of implementing the far-reaching legal mandate it gave itself in this area.

THE COUNTER-TERRORISM COMMITTEE

Of the four Security Council counterterrorism-related bodies, the CTC has received priority attention and resources from the UN as the "center of global efforts to fight terrorism."[15] The committee, which was established in the aftermath of September 11, 2001, has been tasked with monitoring, assessing, and facilitating implementation by states of Resolution 1373. This groundbreaking resolution imposed sweeping legal obligations on UN member states, requiring every country, among other things, to freeze the financial assets of terrorists and their supporters, deny travel or safe haven to terrorists, prevent terrorist recruitment and weapons supply, and cooperate with other countries in information sharing and criminal prosecution. In order to expedite its adoption, the United States cobbled together a resolution that included provisions from the bombings and financing conventions, which the Security Council made binding on all states overnight.[16] However, it did not attempt to define terrorism, leaving each country to apply its own definition, and thus steering clear of the contentious discussions that were going on (and continue to go on) in the General Assembly.

The CTC has sought to focus on the less controversial aspects of counterterrorism, for example by working to strengthen states' counterterrorism infrastructure and enhance counterterrorism cooperation among states and organizations. It stands back from the politically charged discussions of definitions and root causes. It has sought to work with all states to help identify their capacity gaps, to serve as a switchboard between donors and interested states, and to minimize duplication and overlap among potential assistance providers. Significantly, the CTC has received and reviewed more than six hundred reports from member states and is thus conducting the first worldwide audit of counterterrorism capacities.[17]

The CTC has had some success in monitoring implementation. Some states have adopted new or have improved existing counterterrorism legislation, border controls, and executive machinery. For example, the CTC observed that some states thought their anti–money laundering laws to be adequate to address the financing of terrorism. The CTC reminded them, however, that although interrelated, the crimes of money laundering and terrorist financing are not identical and thus may require separate pieces of legislation. As a result, countries like the United Arab Emirates and Kuwait have adopted anti–terrorist financing legislation. In addition, the CTC noticed that many states lacked the appropriate controls over informal banking systems such as *hawala* or *hindi* that have been exploited by terrorists. At the CTC's urging, some states responded with enhanced regulation. Furthermore, partly as a result of the CTC's prodding, the number of countries that are party to all international terrorism treaties has risen from two in September 2001 to more than seventy today.

In addition to working with states, the CTC has reached out to some sixty international, regional, and subregional organizations to encourage them to become more involved in the global counterterrorism campaign—for example, by developing counterterrorism action plans, best practices, and units within their secretariats, while urging their members to join the international terrorism–related treaties and implement Resolution 1373.

For the first two and a half years of its existence, the CTC's work was supported by a handful of consultants (many former UN diplomats with little relevant experience) hired by the UN Secretariat on short-term contracts. Given the breadth and long-term nature of the CTC's mandate, it became clear that a larger, more permanent and professional staff body would be needed. The Security Council created such a body, the Counter-Terrorism Committee Executive Directorate (CTED), in March 2004. After lengthy delays due principally to the cumbersome UN budget and personnel processes, the CTED, with its twenty experts, became fully staffed in fall 2005, more than eighteen months after it was created. With this larger group of experts, the CTC is now able to send teams to countries to assess their on-the-ground efforts to implement Resolution 1373—it has so far visited eight countries—and to begin to determine more effectively the areas in which states need the most help. Neither the CTC nor its CTED have the resources to provide any assistance, however. Thus, even if the CTC can effectively determine the most urgent gaps to be filled, which still remains a big if, it must rely on donors to come forward to deliver the necessary aid.

THE NON-PROLIFERATION COMMITTEE

Motivated partly by a heightened sensitivity to nuclear security after the revelations in February 2004 of the nuclear black market run by Pakistani scientist A. Q. Khan and following the precedent of Resolution 1373, the council adopted Resolution 1540 in April 2004. This requires all states to take a series of legislative and regulatory steps to prevent weapons of mass destruction (WMD) and their means of delivery from getting into the hands of terrorists and other nonstate actors. It further established a committee with a two-year mandate to monitor states' efforts to implement their 1540 obligations and a group of eight independent experts to support the committee's work.[18] On April 27, 2006, the Security Council adopted Resolution 1673 to extend the committee's mandate for a second two-year term.

The committee got off to a slow start due to the presence of Pakistan, which rotated off the Security Council and thus the committee at the end of 2004. Pakistan, which viewed itself as a target of Resolution 1540 and only reluctantly voted to adopt it, tried to use the negotiations of the committee's rules of procedures and guidelines as a way to dilute both its mandate and the impact of the resolution. Although unsuccessful in the end, Pakistan took advantage of the rule that gives every committee member the ability to block any decision from being taken to prolong the negotiations, thus delaying the start of the committee's substantive work by almost six months.

Although state reporting to the committee has lagged, partly because of reporting fatigue among countries burdened with an ever-increasing number of council counterterrorism-related committees to report to, the committee has made some progress.[19] It has begun to identify the different steps states should take to implement fully the provisions of the resolution and to indicate to states what additional steps still need to be taken. Moreover, Resolution 1673 contains a provision calling on the committee to report to the council on compliance with the council-imposed WMD obligations by April 2008.

Nevertheless, the committee's day-to-day work continues to be impeded somewhat by China's insistence that the committee's experts only look at government, rather than all public, sourced material in analyzing a country's implementation efforts, thus limiting the amount of information the experts can use to analyze each country's performance. As demonstrated in the case of Pakistan, the fact that one state's objections can delay, or even paralyze, the process for responding to even the most pressing threats to global security is telling of the easy paralysis of many UN bodies that is endemic within the political organs of the UN, including all of the council's counterterrorism-related ones. This approach, which will likely impede the committee's ability to submit a report on compliance that identifies noncompliant countries by name, will be discussed in chapter 3, and tends to lead to lowest common denominator decisionmaking, which may not be conducive to addressing the global terrorist threat effectively.

THE 1267 COMMITTEE
(AL-QAIDA AND TALIBAN SANCTIONS COMMITTEE)

Although originally established as part of the Security Council's strategy to address the terrorist threat posed by Taliban-controlled Afghanistan, the mandate of the 1267 Committee (which has since become known as the Al-Qaida and Taliban Sanctions Committee) was expanded following September 11, 2001, to deal with the global al Qaeda threat. Thus, it now monitors the implementation of financial, travel, and arms sanctions against al Qaeda, the Taliban, Osama bin Laden, and their associates. As part of its response to the events of September 11, the council required all states to impose these measures on the individuals and entities listed by the committee, which manages and updates the list. To assist the committee with its work, the council established an eight-person Analytical Support and Sanctions Monitoring Team (Monitoring Team) to "collate, assess, monitor, and report on" steps being taken to implement and enforce the sanctions measures against those on the list and to recommend new measures to address the evolving al Qaeda threat.

Today, there are more than four hundred names on the committee's list, the vast majority of which were submitted by the United States in the aftermath of September 11 either alone or in conjunction with other UN member states. In the weeks following that day, according to one Security Council diplomat, "there was enormous good will and a willingness to take on trust any name the U.S. submitted."[20] During this period, the creation of the list was based largely on political trust, with the committee having no particular guidelines or standards for states to follow in proposing names. Since then, the committee has adopted such guidelines, putting minimum evidentiary standards for submitting names and a transparent listing process into place to help ensure that due process and other human rights standards are respected. Yet concerns about the committee's lack of due process continue to dominate discussions regarding its work, with the procedures for listing and delisting proving to be contentious.

Maintaining support for the committee's work and implementation of the sanctions remain high priorities in the global counterterrorism effort. Such support, however, according to council watchers, seems to be eroding as a result of these due process concerns.[21] The committee continues to try to strike the right balance between its European members, which generally favor greater transparency and providing those on the list with more rights, including possibly allowing them to approach the committee directly, and other, less forward-leaning members. Even with the mounting controversy surrounding the process (or lack thereof) for adding and removing names from the list, however, it does still serve as the primary vehicle by which states are empowered to freeze the assets of suspected al Qaeda and Taliban members. Whereas countries may be reluctant to freeze the assets of an entity simply because the United States or another powerful country suspects it of having ties to al Qaeda, they have an obligation under international law to do so if that entity is included on the committee's list.

With respect to state implementation of the sanctions themselves, the record is mixed.[22] As the reports of the Monitoring Team have revealed, the travel ban and arms embargo have produced few tangible results. The asset freeze requirement, as mentioned above, has proved valuable in helping internationalize the policy of freezing terrorist assets.[23] However, despite the success, albeit limited, of the asset freeze, the UN secretary-general's High Level Panel on Threats, Challenges, and Change, the secretary-general himself, and world leaders at the 2005 World Summit noted that too often the UN-imposed sanctions are not implemented and more must be done to ensure that they are. Rather than a lack of political commitment from states, the Monitoring Team has found a lack of legislative and operational capacity to be the major impediment to implementation.

THE WORKING GROUP ESTABLISHED
PURSUANT TO RESOLUTION 1566

The Security Council's response to the seizure of approximately 1,200 hostages and the death of hundreds of children at a school in Beslan, Russia, was emblematic of its broader efforts to address the terrorist threat. The desire to satisfy short-term political objectives of one or more council members overcame the need to develop a coherent council-led UN counterterrorism program.

The Russian Federation, using the council's robust response to September 11 as its benchmark, pushed the council to adopt its strongest condemnation to date of attacks against civilians in Resolution 1566. In fact, only last-minute objections of the two OIC members on the council, Algeria and Pakistan, and the Russians' desire to maintain council unity in its response to terrorism, stood in the way of the council adopting its own definition of terrorism in this resolution and thus treading upon what many UN members view to be within the sole purview of the General Assembly. Many council members, some of which had been victimized by terrorism, wanted to show their solidarity with the Russians, and thus were eager to accommodate the Russian proposals, which had little support on their merits. Most significantly, despite recognizing that the council's three existing terrorism-related committees were having difficulty coordinating and that the council's counterterrorism program needed to be rationalized, the council agreed to establish yet another terrorism-related committee, the working group established by Resolution 1566 (2004). The council provided the working group with a mandate (1) to consider practical measures to be imposed upon individuals, groups, or entities involved in or associated with terrorist activities, other than those on the al Qaeda/Taliban consolidated list, and (2) to look into the possibilities of creating an international fund for the victims of terrorism. It did this despite the fact that many individual council members objected both to the notion of an expanded UN list of terrorists absent a UN definition of terrorism and to the idea of an international fund for terrorist victims.

Predictably, the differences among council members that were subsumed during the negotiations of Resolution 1566 surfaced during the meetings of the working group, which has rarely convened and, not surprisingly, has been unable to reach consensus on any meaningful recommendations. Although one commentator suggested that the working group's 2005 report to the council "would [have] provide[d] a prime vehicle for addressing problems of coherence and overlap" in UN counterterrorism mandates, its report failed to address this question.[24]

THE UN OFFICE ON DRUGS AND CRIME

While the General Assembly and Security Council have contributed to the development of an international normative and legal framework for combating terrorism, a number of UN agencies have become involved in providing counterterrorism-related assistance and training to states. The most significant element of this assistance program is carried out by the UN Office on Drugs and Crime (UNODC), located in Vienna. Its Terrorism Prevention Branch (TPB) was established a few years prior to September 11, 2001. It was only after September 11, however, as part of a broader push to get states to join and implement the UN counterterrorism conventions, that the General Assembly shifted the UNODC TPB's mandate away from producing academic studies on terrorism that were of little practical value in providing states with assistance in the drafting of the legislation needed to implement these conventions. Since 2001, TPB, which now consists of some eighteen full-time staff and ten consultants, has delivered country-specific assistance to more than sixty countries and trained more than six hundred lawmakers and other criminal justice officials on ratification and implementation requirements of the international terrorism–related treaties.[25] With staff and consultants stationed in twelve regional offices and nine country offices around the globe, the TPB has a much smaller presence than the UN Development Programme (UNDP), for example, but it has been able to coordinate quite closely with regional organizations, including by cohosting legislative drafting workshops in different regions. In carrying out its activities, the TPB has sought to collaborate with the CTC and its CTED to develop a complementary and synergistic relationship.

In addition to the TPB, UNODC has a small Global Programme against Money Laundering (GPML) with a handful of staff that provides technical assistance to states to strengthen their ability to implement measures against money laundering and the financing of terrorism.[26] Although established in the late 1990s to address issues related to organized crime, since September 11, 2001, its focus has expanded to address terrorist financing. Like the TPB, the GPML is funded mostly from voluntary contributions from UN member states (as opposed to out of the regular budget) and places mentors in key regions around the globe. There is some overlap between the mandates of the GPML and TPB—for example, both offices provide legislative drafting assistance to help states ratify and implement the Terrorist Financing Convention and to implement the Financial Action Task Force (FATF) anti-money laundering and terrorist financing recommendations. Despite this overlap and the fact that they are located in the same Vienna office building, there is little coordination between the two offices.

UN Efforts to Strengthen and Streamline Its Counterterrorism Program

As the above discussion shows, since the events of September 11, 2001, the UN's counterterrorism program has expanded considerably. It is no longer limited to condemning discrete terrorist acts and setting normative and legal standards, but now includes monitoring of states' efforts to meet these standards and working with states to improve their capacity to fight terrorism. The locus of the UN's efforts has thus shifted away from the General Assembly to the Security Council's four intergovernmental bodies and the four UN staff bodies (three Security Council bodies and the TPB). (See Appendix 1.)

With this expansion and shift, there is a growing concern among UN members about the effectiveness of the UN's counterterrorism initiatives and the lack of coordination among its different components, particularly the Security Council committees and staff bodies. In 2004, Costa Rica and Switzerland mounted an effort to include language in the annual General Assembly resolution on "measures to combat international terrorism," calling for the establishment of a UN high commissioner for terrorism to coordinate the growing number of UN counterterrorism initiatives. This call was echoed during the sixtieth (2005) General Assembly.[27] The proposal was motivated in part by a desire among non–Security Council members to shift the focus of the UN counterterrorism effort back to the more inclusive General Assembly by having the General Assembly take control of the currently council-led counterterrorism program, in particular its staff bodies. In the end, the five permanent members of the council objected to it for just that reason, despite acknowledging that the UN effort could be improved.

The desire for improvement and change was most recently expressed by a unanimous General Assembly in December 2005 when it adopted its annual counterterrorism resolution. This included a request to the secretary-general to propose ways "to strengthen the capacity of the United Nations system to assist States in combating terrorism and enhance coordination of United Nations activities in this regard."[28] After extensive consultations with his Counter-Terrorism Implementation Task Force, the secretary-general released his report in April 2006 with his recommendations to the 191 UN Member States on how to enhance the UN's counterterrorism program.[29] The General Assembly started considering these recommendations in May 2006 and the ball is now in its court to come up with a strategy of its own. The secretary-general urged states to focus their efforts on the concrete, practical contributions that the different parts of the UN system can make in the counterterrorism effort and on improving coordination and cooperation among the twenty-three different parts of the system currently engaged in this effort. Not surprisingly, given the General Assembly's track record in dealing with terrorism-related issues, the global body has gotten bogged down with the same political issues that have prevented it from reaching agreement on a definition of terrorism. With the United States, the EU, Japan, and the rest of the global North favoring the secretary-general's pragmatic approach, many in the global South, including nearly every member of the OIC, have sought to have any General Assembly strategy make an explicit distinction between terrorism and "freedom fighters" and to recognize foreign occupation as a root cause of terrorism.

3.

LIMITATIONS OF THE
UN-LED APPROACH

SHORTCOMINGS OF THE CTC-LED APPROACH

As noted earlier, with the CTC at the center of the Security Council's efforts, there have been some modest successes in increasing awareness of the global nature of the terrorist threat and compiling useful information from the hundreds of country reports that have been submitted. The CTC, however, has not been able to play an effective coordinating role among states and organizations. Its inability to fulfill that function is largely due to administrative and other limitations imposed by operating within the UN in New York, which, perhaps as a matter of political necessity, gravitates toward bureaucratic procedural approaches to the issues it faces in order to maintain an element of predictability and avoid potential political disagreements. As primarily a set of political bodies, or purely a political body in the case of the UN Security Council, the UN is ill-suited to the task of implementing many of the technical aspects of the resolutions it adopts. The most straightforward uncontroversial matters, such as facilitating technical assistance between consenting donors and recipients, have a tendency to get bound up in red tape and sidetracked by seemingly endless political discussions. The UN Security Council's counterterrorism bodies have had difficulty, for example, moving beyond the paper-generating exercise of receiving and responding to state reports.

The fifteen-member CTC, which operates by consensus and generally meets on a weekly basis, has tended to focus more on process than on substance. The CTC has succeeded in gathering a large amount of information on each state's counterterrorism capacity, but it has been less successful in analyzing and verifying the data to identify gaps and work with the donor community to fill them. With the CTED in place, the CTC now supposedly has the capacity to conduct site visits and draw from an array of valuable non-UN sources to assess implementation of Security Council–imposed counterterrorism obligations. However, while the committee has in fact conducted a handful of visits, these have not produced any meaningful results. The donor community has been reluctant to rely on the CTC's assessments or other analytical work. In addition, it has not been able to serve as an effective clearinghouse for technical assistance requests from states and offers from potential donors. It has had difficulty reaching beyond the UN diplomatic community in New York to the technical experts in capitals and other organizations.

Finally, the CTC has not been able to sustain the political support that was generated in the aftermath of the attacks of September 11. While much of this failure is attributable to its lackluster performance, given the limited representation on the committee even a properly functioning CTC would lack the broad representation necessary to maintain international support over the long run.[1] Many of the non-council members who did not have a say in the adoption of Resolution 1373 or in the formulation of CTC policies would continue to feel excluded from the Security Council's counterterrorism program. Thus, even if it were to operate more effectively, these countries would continue to lack a sense of ownership in the program, and this would likely affect their readiness to cooperate with the CTC and other parts of the council's counterterrorism framework.

PROLIFERATION OF COMMITTEES AND DUPLICATION OF ROLES

The proliferation of Security Council counterterrorism programs and initiatives has produced overlapping mandates, turf battles, duplication of work, multiple and sometimes confusing reporting requirements for states, and continuing tension between the Security Council and the UN Secretariat. In general, information sharing and other forms of cooperation between and among these groups have been inadequate, which has inhibited the overall council effort.

There are numerous concrete examples of the ways in which the mandates conflict or efforts are duplicated. In addition to the overlap between the UNODC's TPB and GPML mentioned in the previous chapter, the three that are perhaps the clearest involve, first, the UNODC/TPB and CTC/CTED; second, the CTC/CTED and the Al-Qaida and Taliban Sanctions Committee and its Monitoring Team; and third, the CTC/CTED and the 1540 Committee and its group of experts.

The TPB, while conducting its technical assistance missions, has often ventured beyond issues related to the international conventions and protocols related to terrorism. It has advised countries more broadly about developing counterterrorism legislative capacity and implementing the provisions of Resolution 1373. In doing so, it is delving into issues that lie at the core of the CTC/CTED's mandate. Although this was partly the result of having an understaffed CTED, even a fully functioning CTED will have difficulty controlling the TPB mandate given that it answers to a different parent body. The result is that both the CTC/CTED and the TPB are advising states on how to develop the necessary legislative capacity to implement Resolution 1373. Absent a coordinated message on what steps states need to take, there is a real risk that states will receive different and possibly conflicting messages from different parts of the UN counterterrorism operation. In addition, there continues to be tension between the two staff bodies, stemming mainly from the fact that each draws its mandate from—and thus is accountable to—different UN intergovernmental bodies. Furthermore, the TPB's head reports to the UNODC's director, who is a strong proponent of expanding the UN's Vienna-based activities. A more rational organizational structure would fully integrate the technical assistance and policymaking counterterrorism arms of the organization into a single body with a unified mandate.

The second example involves the duplicative analysis being done by both the CTED and the Monitoring Team in the areas of terrorist financing, arms embargoes, and travel bans. The Security Council–imposed al Qaeda/Taliban sanctions constitute a subset of the measures states are obliged to take under Resolution 1373. Thus, any analysis related to the difficulties of states in implementing the sanctions regime may be relevant to, and duplicative of, analysis related to the difficulties of states in implementing Resolution 1373. This duplication is most apparent in the terrorist financing context, but also applies to the other two areas. In these, the Monitoring Team and the CTED have reached many of the same conclusions, not only as to the nature of the gaps in states' capacity to implement the relevant obligations but also what is needed to fill them. This parallel analysis is generally undertaken with little to no coordination between the two analytical teams, despite the fact that their parent committees report to the same fifteen-state Security Council. The problem is exacerbated by the fact that both the CTED and the Monitoring Team have tended to focus their efforts on the terrorist financing portion of their respective mandates. As a result, there is unnecessary duplication of effort in this field, with few rigorous analyses or assessments being carried out in the other counterterrorism fields.

The third example involves the duplicative analysis being done by both the CTED and the 1540 Committee's group of experts in the areas of weapons of mass destruction. Among its many different provisions, Resolution 1373 includes a couple that are aimed at preventing terrorists from getting their hands on such weapons. Prior to the adoption of Resolution 1540, which is exclusively devoted to this subject, the United States had been pushing the CTC to focus more attention on the WMD-related provisions of Resolution 1373. Despite this overlap in mandates, the CTC and 1540 Committees and their respective staff bodies have yet to agree on a common approach to handling these issues with states.

Another area where there is growing overlap and duplication of effort is in the Security Council's counterterrorism-related outreach to international, regional, and subregional intergovernmental organizations. Since early 2003, the CTC has sought to deepen its relationships with more than sixty different organizations and has attempted to spur them to do more in the field of counterterrorism. Today, both the Al-Qaida and Taliban Sanctions Committee and the 1540 Committee are establishing their own separate contacts with the various organizations as well. Thus, rather than having one Security Council counterterrorism interlocutor with these bodies, which would help ensure the delivery of a consistent message, with many of them there are three. This redundancy puts an increased burden on the organizations, many of which have only one or two people in their secretariats following counterterrorism issues and thus may lack the capacity to engage with one, let alone three, Security Council counterterrorism-related committees in any meaningful way. Representatives from some organizations may also ask themselves why they need to have three different Security Council counterterrorism points of contact.[2]

Many UN members, whether or not they are on the council, believe that the current UN counterterrorism effort is too diffuse and are aware of the lack of coordination that plagues it. Although they have voiced strong support for increased cooperation among the different bodies, in particular the Security Council staff bodies,[3] there have been few improvements to date. Although increased cooperation, if it materializes, might improve the situation somewhat, it will not address the underlying problem of different staff bodies that are unaccountable to each other with separate budgets, different leaders, and overlapping mandates. Thus, absent a formal integration of the multiple staff units into one office under the direction of a single individual who has day-to-day responsibility for ensuring cooperation, the situation is unlikely to improve significantly.[4] This point has been underscored by Simon Chesterman, executive director of the Institute for International Law and Justice at New York University School of Law, who has written that "if only for reasons of efficiency it appears desirable to rationalise these various supporting offices whose mandates are recognised as overlapping."[5]

CHALLENGES FACING THE UN SYSTEM

The enormity of the global counterterrorism challenge contrasts sharply with the inherent political, administrative, and budgetary challenges of operating within the UN system. Even with the integration of the existing council counterterrorism expert bodies into a single unit, there would still only be a team of fewer than forty experts, with an annual budget of less than $14 million (see Table 2.1). These are not sufficient human and financial resources to allow the council to fulfill its broad counterterrorism mandate. For example, the IAEA—the world's central intergovernmental forum for scientific and technical cooperation in the nuclear field, working to verify that safeguarded nuclear material and activities are not used for military purposes—has a staff of some 2,200 people (with more than one-half of them technical experts) and an annual budget of some $268 million.[6]

Because the funding for the UN's counterterrorism programs comes from the regular UN budget, it is subject to the politics of the Fifth Committee, the main committee of the General Assembly responsible for administration and budgetary matters. It must compete in this committee with other important programs for limited resources.[7] Although UN budgets, after a long freeze in the 1990s, are growing by some 20 percent every two years, the Fifth Committee, in which states from the developing world constitute an overwhelming majority, has been reluctant to award additional funds to the counterterrorism programs. The budget negotiations are notoriously contentious and highly political, often pitting developing states' demands for increased funding for the UN's humanitarian, social, and economic programs against developed states' demands for increased funding for counterterrorism and other security-related programs. For example, during the 2004 budget negotiations, a number of developing states objected both to the size of the CTED and its budget request, and thus insisted upon including language in the relevant General Assembly resolution "request[ing] that the Secretary-General, in preparing the next budget proposals for the CTED, to review and consider possible streamlining of the structure and level of positions, bearing in mind its temporary nature and its status as a subsidiary body of the Security Council."[8]

Given the different, and at times competing, priorities of the global North and South and the Fifth Committee practice of reaching consensus on the budget, it is unlikely that the UN's counterterrorism program could ever be allocated the resources needed to succeed so long as it is funded out of the UN regular budget and perceived as a Security Council–led exercise. This is particularly so as time passes and the events of September 11 recede into memory.[9]

The decisionmaking processes of the committees have also presented serious challenges. The practice in all Security Council subsidiary bodies of taking all decisions by consensus has significantly impeded their ability to take action in a timely fashion and at times diluted their work. For example, after more than a full year of discussions, the CTC has still not been able to agree on a set of terrorist financing best practices, which would consist of simply endorsing the work of the FATF, the premier international standard-setting body in the fight against terrorist financing. In contrast, the council, which does not take decisions by consensus (except generally among the five permanent members), needed only three weeks to draft, negotiate, and adopt a resolution (Resolution 1617) calling upon all states to implement the FATF standards. In order to maintain its relevance and effectiveness, the leading multilateral counterterrorism body needs to be able to act quickly and decisively. This is particularly so given the often fast-paced transformations in the global security environment.

The same consensus-based practice has made it difficult for any of the Security Council counterterrorism-related bodies, including the Al-Qaida and Taliban Sanctions Committee, to identify nonperformers ("name and shame") or even to agree on a set of standards against which to measure performance. On a number of occasions, one or two committee members, including the one representing the region in which a targeted country is located, have successfully blocked any efforts to exert meaningful pressure on a particular country. Brazil, for example, opposed putting increased CTC pressure on Paraguay despite the latter's admitted inability to comply with Resolution 1373 due to parliamentary intransigence, blocked a proposed CTC visit to Peru, and generally prevented the CTC from visiting any country in Latin America during its two years on the committee. Furthermore, these rules have impeded efforts within the council's counterterrorism bodies to focus on the more politically sensitive areas of the resolutions. For example, the CTC has been unable to devote meaningful attention to monitoring the implementation of the Resolution 1373 obligation to deny safe haven to terrorists. In practice, the consensus approach has meant that the political and legal power of the different Security Council resolutions on terrorism adopted under Chapter VII of the UN Charter, which authorizes the Security Council to impose far-reaching legal obligations and sanctions on states, and the subsidiary bodies that were created using this same authority are significantly weakened.

Counterterrorism is just one of the many issues with which the Security Council is seized and it has proved difficult to maintain the subject's priority treatment in that forum. Some of the CTC's success in its first two years was attributable to the heightened attention it received from council members (as well as from the rest of the UN membership), with CTC members generally being represented at CTC meetings by senior officials, including sometimes ambassadors, from their missions. The quarterly CTC briefings in the council were well attended, often with some thirty non-council members delivering statements. Since then, however, interest has waned, with the attention of delegations often divided among a number of pressing issues, of which the CTC or terrorism more broadly is only one. With the CTC now seen by many within the UN as a rather technical, paper-processing body, to which there is little urgency of action, second and third secretaries are commonly seen representing their delegations around the CTC table. Furthermore, the quarterly Security Council briefings now attract fewer than a dozen non-council member speakers. In fact, only the EU and seven non-council members took the floor at the most recent such meeting (May 30, 2006), with the majority of the speakers (that is, Cuba, Iran, Israel, Syria, and Venezuela) taking the opportunity to address a particular bilateral alleged terrorist threat rather than the council's role in addressing terrorism.[10] Given the lengthy delays in setting up the CTED, the CTC was operating well below operational capacity for so long that many delegations may have felt the CTC could do little that merited the attention of more senior officials from CTC delegations, let alone non-council members.

The council is generally focused on responding to specific, time-limited threats to international peace and security. Thus, it responds quickly and forcefully to a discrete terrorist incident, meeting at night or on the weekend to adopt the necessary resolution or presidential statement. It has found it difficult, however, to sustain the momentum of its long-term counterterrorism capacity-building program and the multitude of tasks that are involved. Although global events have helped to create the urgency for action that led to the adoption of all of the major Security Council counterterrorism resolutions, and which gave birth to the Security Council's counterterrorism architecture, unrelated crises such as Darfur, Iraq, or the Israel-Palestinian situation have understandably distracted the council's attention from its important ongoing, largely technical, counterterrorism work.

Much of the UN's comparative advantage in the field of counterterrorism lies in capacity building and standard setting, both of which have a significant technical component. Yet, because the UN's work in this area is overseen by the Security Council and its subsidiary bodies, this effort has been and will continue to be heavily (and perhaps unnecessarily) politicized, with delegations often interjecting tendentious political issues, thus slowing down the legal and technical work. Thus, when the Security Council is in the throes of a contentious negotiation outside the purview of its counterterrorism-related committees, the differences of views and even animosities among certain delegations can spill over into these bodies. This occurred in the latter part of 2005, for example, when the council was seized with the assassination of former Lebanese prime minister Rafik Hariri.

This phenomenon is not unique to the council's counterterrorism work. Ambassador Richard Butler, a former executive chairman of the United Nations special commission to disarm Iraq, has written about the inevitable influence of political issues on the Security Council's non-WMD work with Iraq. He points out that "[w]hen the Security Council . . . considered WMD issues, other interests—regional, economic, global, strategic, and political—have distorted its treatment of intrinsically WMD problems."[11] One possible solution, he therefore concluded, was to separate the task of preventing the spread of WMD from the Security Council's other, wider political agenda. Nonproliferation, he argued, "must be made an exception from politics as usual." Since Butler published these remarks in 2003, the council, by establishing the 1540 Committee, has tried to separate its WMD work from other council business. Yet this has not discouraged states from raising often unrelated political issues in the context of the council's work in this area.

The problem of overpoliticization of technical issues is exacerbated by the fact that the representatives on the CTC and other Security Council counterterrorism-related bodies are usually political officers (regular diplomats or generalists), often with little or no background in the technical field of counterterrorism. As a result, rather than focusing on concrete country, regional, or thematic issues, the bodies, in particular the CTC, have tended to become unnecessarily consumed in negotiating process-oriented papers and focusing on the political rather than the technical aspects of a particular issue. This is in contrast to technical organizations such as the IAEA, the Organisation for the Prohibition of Chemical Weapons (OPCW), Interpol, and ICAO, where member state delegations generally include domestic experts in the relevant field. For example, the U.S. delegation to the IAEA includes representatives from the Department of Energy, its delegation to the ICAO includes representatives from the Federal Aviation Administration, and its delegation to the World Customs Organization includes representatives from the Department of Homeland Security.

Finally, the principal UN organs in New York, including the Security Council and its subsidiary bodies, are often devotees of precedent, determined to follow established precedents and fearful of setting new ones, which often results in an excess of caution and a fear of trying anything new. This caution is heightened when dealing with issues related to the allocation of responsibilities among the different UN organs under the charter. For example, it took months for the council to establish the CTED as a unit within the UN Secretariat funded out of the regular UN budget, with its executive director appointed by and reporting to the council (or the CTC), largely because the council had never done anything quite like that before and some council members (as well as the UN Secretariat) were concerned that this would set a precedent for dealing with future council issues.[12] This fear led Pakistan, Brazil, and Germany, among others, to insist on including language in the resolution establishing the CTED that explicitly recognizes the uniqueness of the situation. This recognition was intended to signal that creating a special secretariat body to staff a particular council issue was a one-time event and should not be repeated. This fear of setting a precedent for other council work has also been partly responsible for the CTC's reluctance to reach out to the development and human rights communities, including non-governmental organizations in those areas; some of the council's leading members, including the United States, do not want to set any precedents for formal NGO involvement in Security Council activities, debates, and decisionmaking. Given the rapidly evolving nature of the terrorist threat, it is important that the body that is supposed to be coordinating the multilateral, nonmilitary counterterrorism effort has the operating flexibility it needs to adjust to the threat and make decisions without having to worry about establishing a precedent that might not be welcomed in nonterrorism contexts. Neither the CTC nor any of the other council counterterrorism-related bodies currently has this luxury.

Monitoring the implementation of states' counterterrorism obligations requires a long-term and unwavering commitment—one that will not diminish as the memories of the most recent horrific terrorist attack fade or if the Security Council is seized with specific threats to international peace and security that require its urgent attention. It might take some states decades to develop their infrastructure to be able to implement fully the counterterrorism obligations imposed by the Security Council and international treaties. Given the importance and long-term nature of the task, and the above-mentioned political and institutional limitations of working within the UN, serious consideration should be given to studying alternative models to the current approach, including the establishment of a dedicated counterterrorism organization outside of the UN.

4.

Possible Short-term Improvements
Making the Current Security
Council–led UN Approach to
Combating Terrorism More Effective

Although not going as far as the Costa Rican and Swiss proposals mentioned in chapter 2, some or all of the core elements of the UN counterterrorism program could be consolidated in order to make it more coherent and effective. Consolidation would not address the political and institutional limitations of operating within the UN, but it would improve the situation somewhat and need not consume significant time and energy. It could be pursued in the short term while states give careful consideration to the question of whether a global counterterrorism organization, either within or external to the UN system, is needed and, if so, how to go about creating it.

Indeed, a report released in March 2006 by the UN secretary-general, as follow-up to the outcome of the Millennium Summit in 2000, takes note of the fact that there is overlap between the three existing counterterrorism subsidiary bodies of the Security Council and the expert groups. The report therefore urges the Security Council to consider in the near term "ways to consolidate the separate reporting obligations of the three bodies into a single one."[1] In addition, the secretary-general's report calls for efforts to bring experts from all three bodies into a single combined country mission and to "think about a universal procedure for addressing noncomplying States." Finally, the counterterrorism-related section of the report concludes that, in the "long run, it would be a good idea to look at the possibility of creating a single subsidiary body that covers all the expertise of the current three. This body could include experts in different areas and would in effect take care of the other problems mentioned. Of course the implementation of any of these recommendations would require a special resolution of the Security Council."

Although the secretary-general's report refers to two possible forms of consolidation, three such options exist: consolidation that is (1) limited to Security Council staff bodies; (2) broader in scope, also integrating the experts in the UNODC's TPB and GPML; or (3) combined with either of the first two options, consolidating the existing Security Council intergovernmental bodies related to terrorism into a single member state committee. The Gingrich/Mitchell Task Force on UN Reform, finding the UN counterterrorism program poorly coordinated, recommended that some of these options be explored.[2]

Any of these consolidations can and should be carried out in conjunction with two other reforms, which would enhance the council's efforts and build support from non-council member states, particularly the smaller ones: the consolidation of the multiple reporting requirements into a single requirement and consolidated country visits by the various groups of experts. States would submit one report to the council, on a periodic basis, that contains efforts to implement all of the Security Council–imposed counterterrorism mandates. By addressing the reporting fatigue complaint head-on in this way, the council would eliminate a reason (or excuse) more and more states are giving for not cooperating fully with the various counterterrorism-related bodies. In addition, as recently confirmed by the Japanese permanent representative to the UN, consolidated site visits would enhance the effectiveness of the dialogue between the various council counterterrorism mechanisms and government officials and improve the information gathering and sharing. The "rationalization of visits would [also] relieve the burden on visited states."[3]

There would likely be strong support within the UN community for an integration of the Security Council staff bodies while preserving the integrity of the separate council committees. A wide range of UN members, including both members and nonmembers of the Security Council, recognize that cooperation and coordination among these groups remains inadequate and that the resulting duplication of effort and overlapping mandates are hampering its counterterrorism performance. The criticisms of the current diffuse approach are not limited to members of the global North. In fact, it is the members of the global South that have perhaps been more critical of the current setup.[4] Many have had difficulty distinguishing among the different mandates of the Monitoring Team, the CTED, and now the 1540 Committee Group of Experts; they are inundated with multiple, seemingly duplicative reporting and other requirements. Furthermore, there is awareness within the UN community that the repeated calls from the Security Council for enhanced cooperation, including the drawing up of a single, unified work plan and coordinated site visits, have gone unheeded. Finally, with reform at the top of most countries' UN agendas in 2006, the idea of consolidating the UN bureaucracy to make it more efficient and effective should resonate both in New York and in world capitals.

Ultimately, because this consolidation requires action only by the Security Council and does not affect any existing General Assembly–mandated activity, the council should be able to carry this out with little difficulty, particularly since the mandates of the different council intergovernmental subsidiary bodies would not be affected. The UN Secretariat, which has never fully embraced deepening its involvement in counterterrorism issues, partly because of divisions among UN members and a resulting lack of understanding of what role the UN Secretariat might play in this field, is unlikely to be an impediment to this effort; consolidation would reduce its already limited role in this area.[5]

Most of the opposition to this type of consolidation would center around three factors. First, the uneven and largely untested performance of the CTED to date might make some states leery about giving it added staff and responsibilities. Second, given the lengthy delays in getting the CTED established and fully operational, council members may be reluctant to embark on yet another restructuring of its counterterrorism program. Finally, there is a perceived need to maintain the distinction between Security Council counterterrorism capacity-building and sanctions efforts and between its counterterrorism and WMD efforts.[6]

Yet these differences may not be significant. Many states see the CTC and the Al-Qaida and Taliban Sanctions Committee as having distinct roles and approaches: one is supposed to be a sanctions body with teeth (that is, punitive), and the other a capacity-building body (that is, incentive based). At the end of the day, however, both committees are charged with monitoring the implementation of similar obligations imposed by the Security Council under Chapter VII of the UN Charter. Thus, the same enforcement measures are available for the council to apply against those who fail to comply with the obligations, whether created by Resolution 1373 or one of the al Qaeda/Taliban sanctions resolutions (for example, Resolution 1526 or 1617). The issue becomes whether each committee will submit to the council a list of states that it has determined are not complying with their obligations, and whether the council will decide to take advantage of the available enforcement measures to induce compliance. At this stage, neither body appears close to reaching agreement on the standards to measure states' performance, let alone on a list of the nonperformers and whether to submit such a list to the council.

A second possible consolidation would involve combining the council staff bodies and the UNODC's TPB and GPML into a single unit, thereby formally integrating the technical assistance provision arm of the UN program into the broader capacity-building functions. As both the TPB and GPML have field offices and/or representatives in a number of countries in Africa, Asia, and Latin America, this consolidation would give the Security Council's counterterrorism program a more permanent on-the-ground presence that would enhance its global capacity-building efforts.

As with the first possibility, this unit would support the work of and receive policy guidance from the different Security Council counterterrorism-related bodies. The TPB and GPML, which could be combined as part of this consolidation, could continue to be based in Vienna, with their heads reporting to the head of the CTED in New York rather than the executive director of the UNODC in Vienna. Their mandates, however, would be set by the council rather than by the General Assembly and the UN Economic and Social Council (ECOSOC), as they are currently. Such a consolidation would provide the TPB and GPML with the political clout that comes from being part of a Security Council–mandated staff body when they undertake their legislative drafting and other technical assistance work around the globe.

However, while this form of consolidation makes sense on paper it would be difficult to achieve in practice. Consolidation involving TPB and GPML would require decisions of both the Security Council and the General Assembly. It would involve taking a General Assembly–mandated program—one that receives generally high marks from a diverse group of UN members—and placing them under the authority of the Security Council. Given the growing tensions between the General Assembly and the Security Council over the latter's ever-increasing counterterrorism portfolio, there would likely be considerable resistance among non-council members to bringing the TPB and GPML under the control of the Security Council.

A third possible form of consolidation would combine the four separate Security Council counterterrorism-related intergovernmental bodies into a single committee. This could be done in conjunction with either of the first two. However, it would not be as suitable as a near-term and temporary arrangement as it would likely meet with resistance due to the emphasis that many UN members tend to place on respecting the different mandates of the Security Council subsidiary bodies. Even the Security Council's calls for greater coordination and cooperation among its subsidiary bodies and staff units are balanced with language recognizing the importance of respecting the distinct mandates. The 2005 UN World Summit Outcome Document makes this point as well, encouraging the council to consider ways to strengthen its counterterrorism role, "including by consolidating State reporting requirements, *taking into account and respecting the different mandates of its counter-terrorism subsidiary bodies* [emphasis added]."[7] Although there would likely be support for combining the staff bodies, such support would depend largely on maintaining the mandates of the parent bodies.

Were the council to take the bold step of creating a single counterterrorism committee, it could appoint a committee chair and a vice-chair for sanctions, a vice-chair for WMD, and, if the 1566 Working Group's mandate is extended, a vice-chair for issues being considered by that body. Each vice-chair could convene meetings whenever a particular issue in his/her purview required urgent attention. This would help assuage the fear that the different elements in the council's counterterrorism program would not receive the necessary attention should the council consolidate all of its counterterrorism bodies. A consolidated committee structure could lead to a single council counterterrorism work plan and mandate; this would reduce, if not eliminate, the problems of duplication of work and overlapping mandates that plague not only the council staff bodies but their parent bodies as well.

LIMITATIONS OF SHORT-TERM SOLUTIONS

Although each of these reorganizations would make the council effort more coherent and effective, the Security Council would still be left with a group of only some thirty-five to sixty experts and an annual budget of only about $14 million to $17 million (depending on whether the TPB and GPML were consolidated) to carry out its counterterrorism-related tasks.[8] Thus, the council would still lack the human and financial resources needed to enable it to fulfill its broad mandate and serve as a global coordinator of multilateral, nonmilitary counterterrorism activity. Furthermore, since the council would continue to oversee this effort, the budget would still need to be approved by the Fifth Committee, the hiring of personnel would still need to follow the cumbersome UN rules, and the politicized and process-oriented Security Council counterterrorism bodies would continue to oversee, and thus micromanage, the largely technical capacity-building work of the consolidated staff body. Finally, and perhaps most important, the consolidation would still leave the council, which lacks the broad representation necessary to maintain international support, at the center of the global multilateral counterterrorism effort.

As this brief discussion indicates, these possible consolidations offer only short-term solutions, leaving many of the underlying problems unaddressed. Thus, an entirely new body may be needed.

5.

THE CASE FOR A GLOBAL COUNTERTERRORISM ORGANIZATION

WHERE THE CURRENT SYSTEM FAILS

During and after the cold war, the international community recognized many transnational issues as central to global stability and security. This recognition, along with the widely held view that a multilateral approach was needed to address these issues effectively, led to the establishment of a number of organizations that provide a forum for advancing common goals on these matters and serve as centers of relevant professional expertise (for example, the IAEA and the OPCW). However, despite the global threat that terrorism continues to pose and the increase in counterterrorism activity worldwide, this issue remains one of the few global, let alone security, issues that does not have a dedicated international body.[1] The need to fill this lacuna in the international system has become more apparent with the continuation of terrorist attacks around the globe; the proliferation of counterterrorism programs and initiatives at different levels and in different substantive areas since the events of September 11, 2001; and the UN's uneven performance in this field.

Since September 11, 2001, counterterrorism has become a growth industry, with more and more counterterrorism programs being initiated at different levels and in different substantive areas. During this period, regional organizations such as the Asia-Pacific Economic Cooperation (APEC), the African Union (AU), the Organization of American States (OAS), the Organization for Security and Co-operation in Europe (OSCE), and the Pacific Islands Forum (PIF) have adopted counterterrorism action plans and/or established dedicated counterterrorism units within their secretariats to work with their members in building capacity. Functional international bodies and organizations such as the FATF, the ICAO, the International Maritime Organization (IMO), and the World Customs Organization (WCO), to name just a few, have also added a counterterrorism component to their work. Some have adopted counterterrorism-related best practices, codes, or standards and/or provided training and other forms of counterterrorism technical assistance.

Although improved regional and functional responses should be applauded, most of the organizations are toiling on small pieces of territory or within a narrow field. This piecemeal approach has left swaths of territory (for example, the Middle East and North Africa, Sub-Saharan Africa, South Asia, and former Soviet states) and substantive functional areas (for example, terrorist safe haven, travel, and misuse of the Internet and other media) not covered by an effective multilateral body. It is in these areas where the terrorist threat may be greatest, with states often lacking the capacity—for example, appropriate legal and intelligence infrastructures and land, port, and airport security—to confront the threat posed by home-grown terrorist groups and/or recruited radical Islamists.

As within the UN, the plethora of counterterrorism programs outside it has led to overlapping mandates and lack of coordination and information sharing among the different organizations as well as gaps in regional and thematic coverage. This in turn has led to a growing need and calls for greater cooperation and coordination among the organizations to create more synergy and minimize duplication of effort. For more than four years, the CTC has sought to assume the global coordinating role among organizations involved in counterterrorism. Yet, apart from the convening of four international meetings that brought together representatives of more than sixty international, regional, and subregional organizations as well as encouraging increased counterterrorism efforts by all organizations, the CTC has not made a significant or enduring contribution in this area. For example, although each of the four international meetings concluded with the adoption of an ambitious declaration outlining the areas in which the CTC and other organizations would seek to enhance cooperation,[2] most of the commitments remain unfulfilled. In addition, the CTC has not been able to develop close and responsive relationships with many of these organizations, which has led to difficulties in cooperating to bring technical assistance to states in need. The UN has been unable and is unlikely to be able to coordinate effectively the efforts of the relevant organizations. In the end, it may be that only a dedicated multilateral counterterrorism body—one unencumbered by the UN's political and institutional limitations—will be capable of assuming this important role.

A global body may be needed not just to improve the coordination and cooperation among and effectiveness of the different organizations, but among the states as well. Achieving many goals in the international fight against terrorism (for example, capacity building, norm building, information sharing, law enforcement, and judicial cooperation) requires a level of coordination among and commitment from states that has not yet been reached and is not likely to be reached under the current patchwork arrangement. The CTC's mandate is broad enough to allow it to play this role. The Security Council has asked it to develop the capacities of all states to fight terrorism, to identify gaps and work with assistance providers to fill them, to develop global counterterrorism best practices, to improve bilateral and multilateral information sharing, and to deepen law enforcement and judicial cooperation. The CTC, however, neither has nor is likely to receive the resources nor the broad political support from states to allow it to fulfill this ambitious mandate.

In 2003, the G8 created the Counter-Terrorism Action Group (CTAG), intended to coordinate the delivery of global counterterrorism assistance. Yet the CTAG, like the G8 itself, is an ad hoc political mechanism with no permanent secretariat. It lacks the legitimacy in the global South to enable it to assume a role in both setting global standards and coordinating global multilateral, nonmilitary counterterrorism efforts. It has yet to deliver the results G8 leaders thought it would when they established it at the G8 summit in Evian, France. In short, according to a senior U.S. State Department official, "We have yet to devise a consistent [multilateral] framework to effectively address the numerous gaps that continue to exist between what we can do and what we need to do."[3] A strong multilateral institution designed for and dedicated to combating terrorism worldwide, however, could do so, providing the impetus necessary to encourage states to act.

Such a body could have local offices in key regions around the globe. This permanent, on-the-ground presence would enable it to develop a deeper understanding of the threats, needs, and perspectives of the different regions, something that the current Security Council–led counterterrorism program lacks. These regional offices could also provide much-needed support and mentoring, helping regional organizations to implement effective counterterrorism programs aimed at helping states to implement the international counterterrorism framework. Furthermore, building on the ICAO model, these regional offices could serve as hubs for counterterrorism training programs in the region, thus possibly enhancing the coordination among the various efforts in this area.

AN INCLUSIVE, GLOBAL APPROACH

The perception that the global North dominates the worldwide counterterrorism campaign threatens to undermine it, including the UN's Security Council–led effort. In addition to bringing sustained coordination and focus to the multilateral, nonmilitary counterterrorism effort, a global body that has the support from countries struggling to combat terrorism on their territories—for example, Malaysia, Indonesia, and the Philippines, as well as all European and other developed states—would, to the extent possible, remove the "Made in America"[4] label that many countries have attached to the post–September 11 international counterterrorism effort. It would also help change the perception that this campaign is driven by the global North (for which counterterrorism is more of a priority), which is seeking to impose its security-focused agenda on the global South at the expense of development and fighting poverty (which are generally the South's highest priorities). Furthermore, it would be able to adopt a more holistic approach to countering terrorism than the security-focused one being taken by the current council-led effort. Thus, it might be able to be more responsive to the calls emanating largely from the global South to address the so-called root causes behind terrorism, for example injustice and poverty. Thus, rather than having a limited constituency, as the UN's Security Council–led approach has, a global body and the process of forming it could produce a broad international constituency that recognizes the global nature of the problem while creating a structure designed to address it effectively.

Finally, creating a global counterterrorism body and staffing it with independent, technical experts would help depoliticize the current UN Security Council–led effort. Removed from the highly political Security Council environment, where council members have repeatedly sought to micromanage and inject often extraneous political issues into the work of the council's counterterrorism staff bodies, the new body's technical experts could operate more freely, with only broad oversight from the body's member state governing board. Largely unencumbered by the political and process-oriented approach that defines the Security Council–led effort and tends to impede the work of the counterterrorism staff bodies, the experts could more easily identify and promote best practices, set standards, and create objective metrics for evaluating states' efforts.

Much of the work that needs to be done to improve global, nonmilitary counterterrorism coordination among states and organizations and to improve their counterterrorism capacities is technical and not political. Thus, it makes sense to give the lead role in coordinating these intergovernmental efforts to a body that is technical in nature and sufficiently insulated from the day-to-day politics of the UN's political organs. This will allow it to carry out its work effectively and efficiently while still having a far-reaching mandate.[5]

6.

WHAT A GLOBAL COUNTERTERRORISM ORGANIZATION COULD CONTRIBUTE TO THE FIGHT AGAINST TERRORISM

Whether directly connected to the United Nations or as a stand-alone entity, a dedicated counterterrorism organization could take over the work of the four existing Security Council counterterrorism-related bodies, particularly the CTC, plus the TPB. This new organization could focus and build upon their work.[1] It could be charged with monitoring the implementation not only of the Security Council–imposed counterterrorism obligations, including the al Qaeda/Taliban sanctions, but the nonproliferation obligations as well. In addition, it could provide, rather than simply facilitate, technical assistance, including through the establishment of a technical assistance trust fund.[2] Freed from the limitations of the UN's political bodies, it could more effectively perform these tasks.

The counterterrorism-related work of organizations in the broader UN family would be unaffected, except insofar as a new global body would enhance the cooperation and coordination among them. Some states might initially balk at transferring the responsibilities for monitoring the implementation of Security Council counterterrorism obligations to a new, non-council body for fear that such a body would not be as powerful as those under the Security Council, lacking as it would the council's enforcement capacity. For reasons explained earlier, however, none of the council's counterterrorism bodies are able to make use of the council's authority and influence; for example, they are unlikely ever to identify nonperformers, let alone be able to refer a country to the council for enforcement action. Further, the current approach of operating under a robust Chapter VII mandate has impeded the efforts of the CTC to cooperate with technical assistance bodies such as the IMF and UNDP, which are concerned about having their work become unduly politicized. While there would be a number of benefits from no longer being part of the council, the new organization could also retain some link to the council, for example the authority to refer states to it for remedial action. Thus, no real loss of power or authority need result from such a transfer.

This new organization could take a more comprehensive approach to combating terrorism, in part by ensuring more rigorous analysis of states' capacities, identification of what states' priorities should be, and a more proactive approach to working with states and organizations. This enhanced analysis and action could be used to address states' lack of capacity and difficulties in implementing the myriad counterterrorism-related obligations in a more effective manner, reducing the current overlap of the expert assessments being done by both UN and non-UN bodies and more efficiently utilizing limited resources. The priorities of a new organization would be clearly defined so that achievable goals could be set. It would focus on assessing and monitoring states' efforts to implement a series of counterterrorism-related obligations, which could be drawn from existing council ones, and to join and implement the thirteen international conventions and protocols related to terrorism. If the General Assembly is able to finalize the Comprehensive Convention on International Terrorism, and thus reach agreement on a definition of terrorism, a global body could also be given responsibility for monitoring the implementation of this instrument.

Fulfilling these mandates could involve a number of functions and could be carried out free from the limitations that bog down the current UN effort. First, a new counterterrorism agency could adopt and propagate a series of standards and best practices by borrowing from existing, generally underdeveloped, criteria and organically developing others in areas where none exist. Despite the vast amount of counterterrorism activity being carried out in both the UN and in other international bodies, formal standards for evaluating state capacity and performance in implementing UN-imposed counterterrorism obligations do not exist and are unlikely to be developed given the heavily political environment in which the Security Council bodies operate, despite the calls from the secretary-general in his report on "recommendations for a global counterterrorism strategy" for the development of such standards.[3] The creation of evaluation criteria would benefit states as they seek to implement counterterrorism requirements by enabling them to see a light at the end of the tunnel. Such criteria would also benefit regional organizations seeking to persuade their members to improve their counterterrorism capabilities. In addition, they could serve as an incentive to encourage further implementation efforts by states, as they would provide a road map for the steps that need to be taken to implement the various international counterterrorism obligations. In so doing they would play a major role in ending the current situation of continuous exchange of information between the CTC and other UN counterterrorism-related bodies and officials in capitals, a system under which no one has a clear understanding of when or how the process will be completed.

Second, a specialized counterterrorism body, if provided the necessary operational capacity, human and financial resources, and appropriate array of technical expertise, could conduct credible and comprehensive assessments of the counterterrorism capacity of states. Relatively few countries have the necessary legal, administrative, and regulatory capacities to freeze terrorists' assets, monitor the formal and informal banking systems, prevent the travel of designated individuals, deny safe haven to terrorists and their supporters, and suppress the recruitment and military supply of terrorist groups. Many states face deficiencies in their operational and administrative capacity for combating terrorism. By providing up-to-date information about states' capabilities and needs, with a clear set of priorities for each state, the new body would enhance global technical assistance efforts and secure its central role in the international, nonmilitary counterterrorism effort. It would monitor implementation of the myriad obligations and standards and ensure that states that lack the capacity are linked up with available assistance.

In addition, an effective and broadly representative global counterterrorism body could help shoulder the capacity-building and training burden currently undertaken by a handful of states and organizations. In the area of terrorist financing, for example, the

United States, because of diminishing resources due to the heavy costs of training Iraqi and Afghan officials, focuses its technical assistance efforts on some twenty priority countries it believes are the most vulnerable. A global body could focus on those countries that are not priority countries for the United States or the other major donors (for example, the European Union or the CTAG).

Furthermore, a global body with broad North-South support could take the lead in working with those countries in which the major donors lack the necessary access and leverage to push for the enhancement of counterterrorism capacity. Assuming it had regional offices, these could be used as platforms for capacity-building efforts such as training programs at the regional level. Using this type of framework for training would be particularly valuable in regions where a U.S. or other Western capacity-building effort might not be welcomed. This approach, as opposed to bilateral training programs, would also be valuable as it would bring together officials from a group of countries in a region or subregion and allow them to develop relationships essential to promoting law enforcement and other cooperation.

Third, a specialized organization could coordinate with regional and functional organizations to conduct on-the-ground assessments and provide legislative drafting and infrastructural development assistance. Effectively coordinating the counterterrorism efforts of international, regional, and subregional organizations requires sufficient staff and resources to convene meetings and workshops of domestic counterterrorism experts to exchange information, share best practices, and report on challenges being faced in the fight against terrorism. The global body could perform the important function of working with regional organizations to help them establish priorities and develop programs and projects. It could then ensure that the lessons learned from a particular project carried out in one region are shared with other regional organizations interested in the issue. To date, not only do the different regional organizations set their own priorities with little regard to what has been or is being done by others, but there is no mechanism to share lessons learned. There is no reason, for example, why a successful border security program in one region should not be replicated in others facing similar threats and capacity problems, while taking into account cultural or other regional differences.

In addition to sharing information regarding regional counterterrorism initiatives, the global body could serve as a central authority to facilitate the sharing of evidence among domestic judicial authorities, mutual legal assistance among prosecutorial authorities, and the implementation of extradition requests. Finally, this new body could examine existing and new ways for law enforcement and judicial authorities to cooperate more effectively.

Fourth, the global body could develop a system for dealing with noncompliant or nonperforming states. This compliance function could take a variety of forms. For example, it could include a mechanism that would allow it to refer states to the Security Council that have failed to comply with a predetermined set of obligations (for example, existing Security Council–imposed obligations or those under the international conventions and protocols), despite reasonable and active attempts to assist them in doing so.[4] A specialized body would only refer those states that it judges lack the political will to implement the obligations.[5] The new body would also need to develop other methods, short of Security Council referral, for dealing with noncompliant states. For example, it could follow the FATF approach and publicly identify such states (that is, "name and shame").

The organization would not only deal in noncompliance, but also develop incentives to encourage states to adopt effective measures against terrorists and terrorist organizations, serving as a conduit for technical assistance. This function would necessarily encompass measures that fall in an area between facilitating assistance and reporting noncompliance to the Security Council. The new body could use the promise of removal from the noncompliant list as an incentive for states to take the necessary actions. Rather than having to conform to the rules and practices of an existing organization, which makes it next to impossible publicly to identify nonperforming or noncomplying states, the founding members of a new global counterterrorism body could design a structure and establish rules and procedures that facilitate achieving this objective. This was done by the founding members of FATF.

A global, dedicated counterterrorism organization would not only be able to carry out more effectively and efficiently the tasks currently being performed by the existing UN bodies; it could also undertake additional tasks. It could respond to Security Council requests to investigate or visit particular countries of concern. It could develop a system to measure states' performance and encourage donors to require states to meet certain minimum standards to be eligible for various forms of non-counterterrorism-related assistance.

A permanent global counterterrorism body, staffed with a full complement of highly trained and experienced counterterrorism experts, could address the most topical and emerging terrorism issues—such as incitement, bioterrorism, cyberterrorism, and terrorism and the media—which do not fit naturally within the purview of any existing multilateral forum. A larger, more expert global organization could also be mandated to propagate counterterrorism methodologies and technologies. A new entity could help to follow trends, as the World Health Organization (WHO) does with regard to potential epidemics, in order to develop global solutions to global problems. The most common procedure to address such changes today is for the General Assembly to discuss them and/or the Security Council either to establish a new subsidiary body to deal with an issue or, as in the case of terrorist incitement, refer it to the CTC.

Finally, a new body could be tasked with considering the thorny issue of root causes. Despite the fact that many UN members believe that a multilateral discussion of the root causes or facilitating factors of terrorism is needed to address the terrorist threat in a holistic manner, this issue has not been fully considered. In the case of the United States, the reluctance results in part from a fear that such a discussion would be an opportunity for its critics not only to argue that poverty, lack of development and opportunity, and political repression justify terrorism, but also to attack both Israel and the United States for their occupation of the West Bank and Iraq respectively. As noted earlier, there might be less resistance to discuss the issue of root causes in a less politicized, more technical setting that a global counterterrorism organization could provide.

As this chapter indicates, a global counterterrorism body could usefully perform a number of tasks. It need not tackle all of them, however, to make an important contribution to the global counterterrorism effort. An organization that does a few things well is likely to be more successful and respected than one with a broader mandate that lacks the resources or political will to implement it. Furthermore, any discussion of the organization's mandate should be tied to the organization's structure, so that the structure is designed specifically with the effective implementation of the mandate in mind.

7.

WHAT A GLOBAL COUNTER-TERRORISM ORGANIZATION MIGHT LOOK LIKE

POSSIBLE MODELS

The numerous international bodies that have been created in the past fifty years to address security and other global issues offer a range of models to look to when forming a multilateral counterterrorism organization. They fit broadly into three categories: a treaty-based body; an informal, political body; or a UN program. Rather than attempting to identify the right model for a counterterrorism body, this chapter will outline the possibilities. It will then enumerate some of their advantages and disadvantages with respect to a set of interrelated issues (legal, political, budgetary, and structural). These are not exhaustive but are among those that would need to be addressed when establishing a new entity.[1] (See Table 7.1, page 55. See Appendix 2 for descriptions of organizations in each category.)

MODELS FOR A GLOBAL COUNTERTERRORISM ORGANIZATION

TREATY-BASED MODEL

The first broad model is a treaty-based international organization. Existing examples include the IAEA, ICAO, International Labor Organization (ILO), WHO, OPCW, and the International

Organization for Migration (IOM). All were established pursuant to a legally binding intergovernmental instrument that sets forth, among other things, the mandate of the body, the terms for membership, the size and competences of the member state governing body and the technical secretariat, the obligations of the organization's member states, and how the body is to be funded.[2] Such a body could be part of the UN system (as the IAEA, ICAO, and OPCW are) or completely separate from the UN (as the IOM is), and impose legal obligations on its members.

INFORMAL, POLITICAL-BASED MODEL

The second broad model is an informal, political-based organization. Examples include FATF, the Egmont Group, the Nuclear Suppliers Group, the Australia Group, the Missile Technology Control Regime (MTCR), the Wassenaar Arrangement, and most recently the Proliferation Security Initiative. Most of these were established as a result of Western initiatives, many by the G7 or G8, and were later joined by varying numbers of non-Western countries. These bodies are selective and self-standing, with no formal links to the UN. They often were established by a mutually agreed document of generally self-selected founding member states.[3] This document generally established criteria for membership,[4] provided for members to decide whether candidate countries should be admitted as new members, and outlined the mandate of the body.[5] The bodies often use different ways of exerting influence on members and non-members to change behavior. Most do not have technical secretariats but rely on their member state representatives to carry out all aspects of the body's mandate.[6]

UN PROGRAM MODEL

The third model is the UN program model. Examples include UNDP, the UN Environment Programme (UNEP), UN Children's Fund (UNICEF), and the UN Office of the High Commissioner for Refugees (UNHCR). Each was established by a General Assembly or ECOSOC resolution and reports to one or both of those bodies. They are generally governed by member state executive bodies ranging in

Table 7.1 Possible Models for a Global Counterterrorism Organization

Model	Main Characteristics
Treaty-Based Model	• legally binding foundation document imposing legal obligations on members, resulting from multilateral treaty negotiation • ability to support large technical secretariat • not subject to UN's institutional and political limitations • governing body of thirty to sixty members, need not be based solely on equitable geographic distribution • enhanced participation of regional and functional organizations • ability to penalize noncompliers • most likely to have the authority to refer cases/countries to the Security Council
Informal, Political-Based Model	• selective and self-standing group, with no link to UN • nonlegal founding document (e.g., political declaration) resulting from fast-track negotiation • flexible mandate and governing structure • limited capacity to support technical secretariat (generally lacking funding mechanism and international staff) • not subject to UN's institutional and political limitations • ability to "name and shame" nonperformers • unlikely to have the authority to refer cases/countries to the Security Council
UN Program Model	• established by General Assembly and/or ECOSOC resolution • broad political legitimacy • membership on governing board based on equitable geographic distribution • ability to support large technical secretariat • subject to UN rules and regulations • reports to General Assembly and/or ECOSOC • unlikely to have the authority to refer cases/countries to the Security Council

size from thirty to sixty member states operating by consensus, include a large technical secretariat, and are funded largely from voluntary contributions.

ADVANTAGES AND DISADVANTAGES OF INTERNATIONAL MODELS

LEGAL ISSUES

Assuming the membership is broad enough, using a treaty-based model would provide the new counterterrorism organization with a strong legal basis for acting on behalf of the international community. This would bring added legitimacy to the multilateral counterterrorism effort. The founding treaty could include a series of explicit obligations for its members and outline both the structure of and mandate for the organization, including its technical secretariat.[7] To help expedite the treaty negotiating process, the negotiators could seek to incorporate into the treaty the existing Security Council counterterrorism-related obligations and even the obligations under the existing international conventions and protocols related to terrorism.

This process could be accompanied by a council decision to delegate monitoring of Resolution 1373 and other counterterrorism-related resolutions to this new body. Doing so would enable the new organization to assume the mandates of the existing Security Council counterterrorism bodies while still maintaining some link to the council. It would also obviate the need to negotiate a new set of obligations, which could be time consuming as it could become bogged down in politically divisive issues related to the definition of terrorism and the situation in the Middle East.

The other two models would not be treaty-based; thus, organizations based on those models could not impose legally binding obligations on their members. A non-treaty-based body would need to find ways to elicit voluntary compliance with relevant counterterrorism standards. An additional disadvantage is that the Security Council might be less likely to delegate the responsibilities currently held by its existing subsidiary bodies to an organization based on a non-treaty model, as this would mean transferring monitoring responsibilities from bodies established under Chapter VII of the UN Charter to ones with no enforcement powers and no authority to impose penalties for violating the voluntary regime.[8]

Theoretically, under any of the three models the counterterrorism organization could refer noncompliant states to the Security Council for appropriate action. However, the threshold for making such a referral and the willingness of the Security Council to accept a referral from a non-UN body would be problematic. Both the IAEA and OPCW governing bodies, which have the authority to refer countries to the Security Council, are part of the UN family. There is no precedent for giving a non-UN political- or legal-based body the authority to refer cases to the council and for having the Security Council accept such referrals. In addition, the Security Council is unlikely to use its Chapter VII enforcement powers for failure to comply with purely political commitments, as would be the case under either the UN program or the informal, political-based model. Furthermore, the larger and more diverse the governing body, the more difficult it will be to exercise referral powers, as highlighted by the IAEA's recent experience with Iran. In short, there will likely be greater political support for giving a global counterterrorism body power to refer cases to the Security Council if it were established as part of the UN family as a treaty-based UN agency than one of the other two models.

The treaty-based model would also provide both the organization and its staff with a number of other legal benefits. For one, the organization itself would have an international legal personality. This legal standing would provide its member states with a clear wall of separation between them and the organization. Given the politically sensitive nature of some of the work of even a technically focused global counterterrorism organization, there will be instances when its member states might want to hide behind this wall and point to the organization as the actor responsible for carrying out a particular policy or monitoring activity.

Another benefit of having legal personality is that the organization could enter into legally binding agreements with its partner international, regional, and subregional organizations. For many organizations, these agreements are a prerequisite to being able to share information concerning or submitted by a particular state. Such relationships would enhance the new organization's ability to play the coordinating role among international, regional, and subregional organizations that the CTC is currently trying but unable to perform. Many organizations have found it legally difficult to enter into institutional arrangements with the CTC and other Security Council bodies that lack legal personality, which is necessary to enhance certain forms of cooperation and coordination. Furthermore, a treaty-based organization would provide its technical secretariat officials with the privileges and immunities necessary to carry out their work without fear of arrest or prosecution by local authorities; the latter might otherwise use such tactics to intimidate the organization from investigating counterterrorism practices.

Like a treaty-based body and existing UN programs, a counterterrorism organization established as a UN program could have the legal personality necessary to hire staff. In addition, both the organization and its staff could receive the privileges and immunities necessary to carry out their work. Under an informal, political-based model, however, absent a special arrangement with a treaty-based institution, neither the organization nor its secretariat would have any privileges or immunities to enable them to conduct their work effectively.

POLITICAL ISSUES

States parties to a treaty creating a global counterterrorism body would likely feel the greatest sense of ownership among the three models because of the broad-based process of international negotiation that would go into reaching agreement on such a document. This would increase the prospects of participation and consent in the organization, and it might generate greater political commitment to implement international counterterrorism obligations. This is in contrast to the present situation, in which some non-council members feel that the UN counterterrorism program was imposed upon them by the Security Council, circumventing the traditional international law-making process.

A treaty-based organization need not be subject to the political and institutional limitations that impede the UN's counterterrorism program. For example, it would not need to use the consensus-based decisionmaking approach that pervades the Security

Council subsidiary bodies. Freed from this limitation, the new body would be more likely to develop criteria for measuring performance, to identify nonperformers, and to adopt punitive measures against them.

It is worth noting that negotiating a multilateral treaty can be a lengthy process. It can take years, if not decades, to finalize and enter into force, let alone attract the level of participation required for broad legitimacy.[9] This process could be particularly difficult in this case as it would involve the politically charged issue of terrorism. It is possible, however, that much of the contentious negotiating could be avoided if negotiators agreed to limit the obligations of states parties to existing Security Council counterterrorism-related obligations and those contained in the existing international conventions and protocols related to terrorism, plus any subsequently adopted by the General Assembly or the UN specialized agencies that enter into force. The negotiators could accept existing resolutions and conventions and focus instead on the institutional/administrative issues related to empowering a new organization.

In addition, the treaty could be negotiated in a number of possible forums, the choice of which could have an impact on the length of the process. For example, a negotiation in the 191-member General Assembly, which has a tradition of adopting treaties by consensus, is likely to last much longer than one among a smaller group of like-minded states in a forum such as the Organisation for Economic Co-operation and Development, the G20, or an ad hoc negotiating forum of like-minded states.[10] The trade-off here, of course, would be less legitimacy than if the treaty were negotiated in the General Assembly or some other more representative forum.

In addition, if negotiated among the G20 or another small group of states, there would initially be only as many member states as members in the group (assuming all negotiating states ratify the underlying treaty). It could take years for the body to assume a near-to-worldwide membership. Moreover, under this model, a small number of states would need to foot the bill, meaning the financial burden on each one would be greater than if established following the UN program model. Furthermore, it is not clear whether the Security Council, let alone the General Assembly, would endorse or support such a body, which could make it difficult to transfer to it the responsibilities for monitoring the implementation of UN-imposed obligations.

On the other hand, although it is not a treaty-based body, the FATF, which has only thirty-three members, is recognized by the vast majority of UN members as the premier standard-setting body in the fight against terrorist financing. Its work has been endorsed by both the secretary-general and the Security Council. Thus, a similarly structured, but treaty-based, global counterterrorism body—that is, with limited membership, clear criteria for admitting new members, full transparency, and the authority to grade performance—could be created and be effective.

Although neither of the other two models would provide the same legal basis for acting as the treaty-based one, they could nevertheless provide a strong political and moral foundation for assuming the central coordinating role in the multilateral counterterrorism effort. With the informal, political-based model, however, this would depend greatly on the size and diversity of its membership.

Regardless of the number, the self-selected group of states meeting to negotiate the document underlying an informal, political-based organization would feel a sense of ownership in the body established by the process, although it is likely to be less than what would result from the longer and more rigorous treaty-making process. An informal, political-based body could also operate entirely outside the UN framework and it too would not be impeded by the UN's rules, regulations, and other limitations.

Because the negotiations of the founding document of a UN program–based body would take place during the regular course of work of the General Assembly or in special session, it might not provide the negotiators with a special sense of ownership in the end result. In addition, both the negotiations of the founding document and the operation of the body itself would be subject to many of the UN's cumbersome rules, regulations, and process-oriented practices. Creating a global counterterrorism organization following this model would require the adoption, probably by consensus, of a resolution by the 191-member General Assembly.[11] Negotiating and reaching consensus on such a resolution, which would include general elements of the body's mandate, would be a time-consuming and politically divisive exercise. As with many resolutions negotiated in these bodies, there is a high risk that substance would be sacrificed for consensus. Thus, one could end up with an organization the mandate of which would have to be watered down in order to achieve unanimity, something that may not be desirable in the counterterrorism arena.

Furthermore, following this model would create an organization that is heavily influenced by, if not part of, the UN culture and its accompanying political and institutional limitations. Because the entire UN membership would be stakeholders, it would be difficult to move the body beyond the evenhanded approach that characterizes the Security Council's counterterrorism program and prevents the Security Council and its subsidiary bodies from "naming and shaming" nonperformers. An advantage of this model, however, would be that a body negotiated this way would have worldwide buy-in and could not be considered elite or "Northern." Such a body might then have more success than the Security Council subsidiary bodies currently have in getting its members to cooperate with it.

BUDGETARY AND OTHER ADMINISTRATIVE ISSUES

A treaty-based organization would be funded without recourse to the UN regular budget. The members of the new organization would agree on the size of the budget, the scale of assessments, and a mechanism for considering and approving the budget.[12] The members could decide on a budget for counterterrorism based on what home governments are prepared to accept as needed to fulfill the organization's purposes, without counterterrorism being traded off against competing priorities in the budgeting politics of the General Assembly's Fifth Committee. As such, its budget could more realistically reflect what is needed to equip a technical secretariat with the necessary number of experts and areas of expertise to enable the organization to fulfill its global mandate.

In addition, by operating outside the UN regular budget, the new organization would not be required to follow the cumbersome UN rules and regulations, including those related to hiring, which tend to give priority to candidates already inside the secretariat of UN system agencies and to achieving equitable geographical distribution. UN employment regulations are widely accused of making it difficult to hire true experts on an expedited basis and of precluding secondments (loans) of national officials from the governments of member states.

Most of the funding for an organization established under a UN program model[13] and all of the funding for one established under an informal, political-based one would also be independent of the UN regular budget. Thus, many of the benefits that accrue from this financial freedom could apply under those models as well.

The vast majority of informal, political-based bodies do not have a technical secretariat and instead rely on the member state delegations to serve that function. The no-secretariat or minimal-secretariat approaches drastically reduce the organization's apparent costs. However, they reinforce the nonpermanency of the body and may reduce the confidence that states and the general public have in the impartiality and integrity of the judgments or assessments issued. There would be no international civil servant bureaucracy with a vested interest in maintaining jobs and preserving an institution even if it has outlived its purpose. On the other hand, a credible global body would benefit from a large professional staff, independence from national governments' potential control, substantial operational capacity, and institutional longevity to address the large-scale, long-term nature of the global terrorist threat. This is especially true in light of the capacity-building focus of the new body and the inadequacy of current staffing and institutional capabilities within the UN program.

STRUCTURAL ISSUES

Under a treaty-based model, the negotiators could design a governing structure that takes into account the particular needs of a global counterterrorism body. Thus, the new organization could have a governing body of some thirty to forty member states elected for a fixed term by the states parties. This would make it more representative than the fifteen-member Security Council but not so unwieldy as to impede decisionmaking.[14] Moreover, as with some existing treaty-based organizations, the composition of the governing body need not be based on geographic balance alone. Rather, it could reserve a certain number of seats for states that are the top counterterrorism assistance providers.[15] The negotiators could also include representatives of donor and/or regional organizations as observers, with the right to attend meetings of the governing body, thus facilitating their active participation in the work of the new organization. This could go a long way toward increasing the coordination and cooperation among the different intergovernmental bodies involved in the fight against terrorism.

The states parties could (and should) agree to do away with the consensus-based decisionmaking approach of the Security Council counterterrorism bodies and decide to take decisions another way. They could consider a weighted voting system like that which exists in the World Bank, in which each state-appointed director on the governing board is allocated a certain number of votes linked to the size of the appointing state's financial contribution to the bank.[16] They might also devise a system that allows only those states to vote that are parties to all of the international counterterrorism conventions and protocols and have agreed to allow for regular on-site assessments by the organization's experts.

Both of the other two models would also allow for the creation of an appropriately sized governing body that strikes the right balance between being representative and effective and that ensures enhanced participation of relevant organizations.[17] Under the UN program model, however, it would be difficult to provide for such enhanced participation, as UN rules, procedures, and precedents make it difficult for organizations to have an active policymaking role in a UN member state body. In addition, because an organization established following the UN program model would be a creature of the General Assembly and/or ECOSOC, it would be difficult to use anything other than geographic balance as the basis for distributing seats on its governing body.[18] For this same reason, while the members of an informal, political-based international body could choose not to take decisions by consensus, it is likely that a UN program would follow the UN practice of operating by consensus.[19]

An organization based on an informal, political-based model would have a more flexible mandate than either of the other models. This flexibility would be largely due to the fact that its founding document—that is, a political declaration—would likely prove easier to amend than either a treaty or a General Assembly or ECOSOC resolution, which provide the mandates for bodies based on the other models. This flexibility could be necessary to ensure the mandate always reflects what is needed to address the rapidly changing terrorist threat. Such flexibility would also allow the body to be more proactive than those of the other models. Mandates of bodies such as FATF and the MTCR, for example, were quickly adjusted after September 11 to focus more of their attention on counterterrorism.[20] Although the Bush administration consulted the U.S. Senate prior to agreeing to these mandate extensions, formal Senate approval (which can take years and may not always be forthcoming) was not required as it would have been had the Bush administration been seeking to alter a treaty-based mandate.

On the other hand, because a body based on an informal, political model would lack a legal foundation and have no permanent secretariat supporting its work, it is more likely to be subject to the ever-changing political and diplomatic winds in and among its members. Under the informal, political-based model, the body could be quickly dissolved if its members believed it had outlived its usefulness or was no longer effective.[21] In contrast, treaty-based bodies usually have detailed and cumbersome provisions for dissolution in the underlying treaty, and a UN program would probably require its founding body—that is, either the General Assembly or ECOSOC—to take action. Under a body based on an informal, political model, states could decide to lessen or withdraw their political and/or financial support as they grow bored with the issue, even if others still feel motivated to stick to it. For example, since the United States would not have any treaty commitment to support and participate in this body, a new administration or a new Congress whose interest was elsewhere could more easily decide to withhold U.S. support or reduce U.S. participation in the body.

OTHER MODELS

In addition to the three broad models described above, two other approaches, neither of which fits neatly into one of the above models, are worth considering. They have been used to improve coordination in the international community's fight against another of the great threats of the twenty-first century, HIV/AIDS.

First, in 1996, the ECOSOC endorsed the establishment of the Joint United Nations Programme on HIV/AIDS (UNAIDS) as an innovative UN venture that is the main advocate for accelerated, comprehensive, and global action against the epidemic. UNAIDS was established in part to improve the coordination of the different actors in the UN system that had a role to play in fighting HIV/AIDS. It is supported by a technical secretariat and is guided by a Programme Coordination Board, which serves as its governing body and comprises both member states (twenty-two, elected based on regional distribution), UN bodies (for example, UNICEF and UNDP), and nongovernmental organizations (including associations of people living with HIV/AIDS).[22]

Second, the Global Fund to Fight AIDS, Tuberculosis and Malaria was created in 2002. It is aimed at dramatically increasing resources to combat three of the world's most devastating diseases and to direct those resources to areas of greatest need. The Global Fund is a partnership among governments, civil society, and affected communities, completely independent of the UN. Its purpose is to attract, manage, and disburse resources to fight these diseases. It works closely with other multilateral and bilateral bodies involved in these issues to ensure the different programs are properly coordinated. The Global Fund is established as a foundation under Swiss law; it has a technical secretariat and a governing board consisting of representatives from the developing world, the donor community, civil society, and the private sector.[23]

CONCLUSION

Given the sui generis nature of a global counterterrorism organization, the new body will likely draw upon elements from many, if not all, of the models. One of the goals of the international process on the future of multilateral counterterrorism would be to have a broad range of stakeholders discuss the pros and cons of the various possibilities, with a view to recommending the elements of each that should be included in a global counterterrorism body. With the large number and diverse nature of international bodies, this process should bring together both those involved in the creation of and those with expertise working inside of some of these bodies.

Regardless of which model is chosen, a dedicated, global counterterrorism body needs to attract broad support from a cross section of countries in order to obtain the financial and political backing needed to ensure its long-term viability and legitimacy. The next chapters will enumerate some of the different reasons the United States, other developed countries, and the developing world might be attracted to the idea of creating such a body.

8.

WHY THE UNITED STATES AND ITS ALLIES COULD SUPPORT A GLOBAL COUNTERTERRORISM ORGANIZATION

There is growing recognition in the United States that what terrorists do abroad and actions countries take, or do not take, to address the terrorist threat in their own territory or region have great consequences for U.S. national security. It has therefore become increasingly clear, even including to the U.S. Congress, that building the capacities of states to combat terrorism is an essential element of efforts to reduce America's vulnerabilities to terrorist attacks both at home and abroad.

President Bush has stressed on numerous occasions that the global terrorist threat requires a global strategy and a global response.[1] The 9/11 Commission wrote in its final report, "9/11 has taught us that terrorism against U.S. interests 'over there' should be regarded just as we regard terrorism against America 'over here.'"[2] This conclusion has been echoed by both senior U.S. policymakers and nonpartisan reports. For example, the president's homeland security adviser recently stated that "Homeland security is a universal concept: As more partners defeat terrorists and defend their homelands, the security of our own homeland increases."[3] Even U.S. officials perceived as favoring a U.S.-led military response to the global terrorist threat have recently recognized the importance of international capacity building. In briefing the Senate Appropriations Committee on the 2006 Quadrennial Defense Review, Secretary of Defense Donald Rumsfeld said that "to succeed [in the global war on terrorism], it will be essential to help partner nations and allies develop their capabilities to better govern and defend themselves. . . [and] our investments and policies should reflect these new requirements."[4]

WHAT THE UNITED STATES HAS TO GAIN

The United States played an important role at the UN in creating the CTC after September 11, 2001. However, the lack of progress since then as well as growing concerns among U.S. officials and experts about the UN's ability to address security issues has created the need for a more effective multilateral body. This body would: (1) increase international cooperation in the field of counterterrorism technical assistance, including by enhancing existing capacity-building efforts by the United States alone and through the G8's CTAG; (2) assess vulnerabilities and set clear priorities for assistance; (3) share the burden of those capacity-building endeavors with other donors, which may have more influence with some recipients than does the United States; (4) facilitate information sharing in a more efficient manner than the UN has been able to coordinate; and, perhaps most importantly, (5) address issues of noncompliance by setting clear standards and implementing a graduated set of options for dealing with states that are failing to meet their counterterrorism obligations.

This begs the question—often asked in Washington these days—of whether the United States loses more in its own freedom of action than it gains when, as a major power, it entangles itself in a global political and administrative process. On counterterrorism, the balance is clear: the United States would derive more benefit from an effective global body dedicated to counterterrorism than it does from existing multilateral efforts at the UN. A new body, for example, could help shoulder the capacity-building and training burdens, spread among many countries, that currently are undertaken and subsidized by the United States and a handful of other states. It could focus on identifying and correcting vulnerabilities in countries that are not priority countries for the United States, its G8 partners, or the EU, which without prompt attention might risk becoming terrorist safe havens or breeding grounds for terrorism. In addition, it could work with those priority countries with which the United States may lack access or leverage.

• • •

With respect to capacity building, there is obviously not enough money available to ensure that each country has the appropriate infrastructure and expertise to prevent terrorists from getting access to the funds and weapons needed to carry out attacks; to investigate, bring to justice, and deny safe haven to terrorists; and to protect borders, transportation systems, telecommunications networks, and production and storage facilities for hazardous materials. Thus, a clear set of priorities for each region and each country needs to be developed. These priorities need to balance the vulnerabilities and risks, taking into account the available resources. This is currently not being done effectively at the global level.

The 9/11 Commission, as well as numerous other governmental and nongovernmental bodies in the United States, has offered a series of recommendations on what the U.S. homeland security priorities should be. Additionally, the federal, state, and local governments have devoted considerable resources to developing counterterrorism strategies with a clear set of priorities. However, the United States cannot simply identify and fund its own priorities. To the extent that Americans' security against terrorism is interwoven with that of other countries, the United States must work with these countries to identify and fund counterterrorism priorities in every corner of the world. As a senior Treasury Department official said in March 2004, "we have found that our success is also dependent on the political will and resources of other governments."[5]

While some countries and regions have the capacity to identify and implement their counterterrorism priorities, many others still do not. This conclusion was made by the Council on Foreign Relations Independent Task Force on Terrorist Financing, which noted that while substantial progress has been made in many countries, a lack of technical capacity still inhibits the ability of some states to comply fully with their counterterrorism-related obligations.[6] This group includes a number of the countries and regions identified by the 9/11 Commission as likely bases of operation for some of the most dangerous international terrorist networks.[7] A sufficiently resourced global body devoted to combating terrorism would be able to identify the priorities for all those unable to do so and then work to ensure that they were implemented, providing or identifying the necessary technical and financial assistance where appropriate.

Traditionally, the United States has been the world's top provider in total dollars of technical assistance and resources to improve developing countries' counterterrorism capacities. After September 11, 2001, the Departments of State and Defense and reportedly the Central Intelligence Agency (CIA) increased their counterterrorism assistance programs. Over the past couple of years, however, according to the authors of a recent study on the evolving terror threat, "the funding for many of these programs has begun to decline."[8] For example, the annual budget for the State Department's Antiterrorism Assistance Program was reduced from the administration's $133 million request to some $122 million in the fiscal year 2006 Foreign Aid Appropriations Bill.[9] This program, with courses for training dog teams to sniff out explosives, enhancing airport and maritime security, training on hostage negotiation, and crisis management and other skills, is designed to enhance foreign law enforcement capabilities. Programs such as these help train the intelligence services, police, prosecutors, and judges in developing countries where terrorists have taken root.[10] In doing so, they not only enhance the capacities of host countries but enable these governments to better protect U.S. commercial and security interests, as well as Americans who travel or live abroad.

The 9/11 Commission reported, "to find sanctuary, terrorist organizations have fled to some of the least governed, most lawless places in the world."[11] The commission then highlighted six areas that it judged to be terrorist sanctuaries. Yet, if other places lacking capacity are ignored in the absence of better globally coordinated approaches, we may be confronted with a list of new places in five to ten years where terrorists have found sanctuary. This will be true even if the current six priority areas are assisted, for example by strengthening regional law enforcement cooperation.

The commission also devotes considerable attention to the need for the U.S. government to do more to protect itself against terrorist attacks. It calls for enhanced action to cut down on terrorist travel. It also states that, among other things, more should be done to exchange information on terrorists with trusted allies and to raise U.S. and global security standards for travel and border crossings through extensive international cooperation. An effective and reliable global counterterrorism body could play a central role in developing and/or disseminating global border and other security standards and ensuring that states are implementing them. This would relieve the United

States and its allies from this task. Perhaps equally important, it would also give these standards added legitimacy.

In addition to sharing the capacity-building burden with the United States, a global body, which would become the focal point for coordinating international counterterrorism technical assistance efforts, would help the international community make better use of the limited funds and expertise that are available. A senior State Department official recently commented on the need for increased international cooperation in the field of antiterrorist financing assistance.[12] In addition to numerous bilateral assistance programs aimed at combating terrorist financing, the World Bank, IMF, UNODC, FATF, and Commonwealth Secretariat, among others, are all active in that field. This official commented that "we have yet to devise a consistent framework to effectively address the numerous gaps that continue to exist between what we can do and what we need to do."[13] A properly designed and effective global body could help do just that in all areas of nonmilitary counterterrorism.

Moreover, such a body could replicate at the international level what the United States has recently created at the domestic level: an open source center to gather and analyze information from the Internet, broadcasts, newspapers, and other unclassified sources around the world.[14] Intelligence officials have said that government policymakers often underestimate the value of this information "because it lacks the cachet of information gathered by more sensitive methods."[15] There is currently no multilateral or global body collecting, analyzing, and disseminating critical unclassified information to understand better and assist in the development of priorities. Having experts from different regions and cultures sit together to assess public source information will provide a useful complement to any domestic efforts in this area.

Yet, as long as the UN lies at the center of the global, nonmilitary counterterrorism effort, this is unlikely to happen. UN member states have demonstrated a long-standing reluctance to allow the UN Secretariat to develop the capacity to analyze threats in support of Security Council decisionmaking.[16] The one recent exception has been with respect to al Qaeda; the council's Monitoring Team has been charged with reporting on the evolving al Qaeda threat. Yet the irony here is that despite being mandated to report on this threat, the Al-Qaida and Taliban Sanctions Committee has prevented the team from identifying specific states that are either not doing enough to imple-

ment the council-imposed al Qaeda sanctions or are the locus of the
threat. This limitation, which is the result of the committee's consensus approach and a UN political culture that makes it next to impossible to single out problem states, has resulted in watered-down
reports. Moreover, the other council counterterrorism-related staff
bodies have yet to analyze global terrorist trends or threats. Instead,
they focus on monitoring each UN member's counterterrorism performance.

Another advantage of a global body is that it could foster innova-
tion and provide a forum for identifying ways to increase public–private
sector partnerships at the global level. These are a critical element of
the fight against terrorism, since terrorists are increasingly aiming
at "soft targets" and critical infrastructures. The organization could
be structured to allow for private sector participation in its work,
something that is currently not possible in the state-centric world
of the UN Security Council. The September 11 attacks highlighted
the unpleasant reality that terrorists are capable of causing enormous damage to the United States (and, similarly, other developed
countries) by attacking its critical infrastructure—as stated by the
Bush administration, "those assets, systems, and functions vital to
our national security, governance, public health and safety, economy,
and national morale."[17] In the United States, as well as in many
other industrialized countries, some 85 percent of this infrastructure is in private hands.[18]

The situation of multinational oil companies with operations in
Nigeria and the Middle East illustrates the problem. Security concerns have led these companies not only to employ their own private
security forces, but, in certain cases, to avoid sending employees into
the regions.[19] As the Center for Strategic and International Studies
reported in October 2005, these concerns "have global ramifications:
as companies have less incentive to invest in new areas, the result
will be lower global oil output."[20]

Given the number of multinational companies and the global
nature of the economy, it is not enough for the Department of
Homeland Security and its European counterparts to energize and
coordinate their respective national efforts to protect critical infrastructure. An attack on such infrastructure almost anywhere around
the globe could have devastating ripples into the U.S. economy. Thus,
Americans should be eager to see similar efforts undertaken by other
countries. They should also welcome the creation of a mechanism, as

part of a global counterterrorism body, for developing and sharing best practices and lessons learned in this area that encourages and allows for the appropriate participation of the private sector. Such participation is incompatible with the existing UN Security Council–led arrangement.

Finally, perhaps the key to obtaining U.S. support for the establishment of a global body devoted to counterterrorism is that such a body, if designed properly, would not only be able to set global counterterrorism standards, but to identify the noncompliers. That is, it would single out those that have or could be provided the capacity to implement those standards but for political reasons remain unwilling to do so. The focus to date at the UN has been on capacity building, with no appetite for any discussion of compliance. So far, none of the council's counterterrorism bodies have recommended the "naming and shaming" of any noncompliant, let alone underperforming, state. Given the consensus rules under which they operate and the tendency of council members to protect their friends and neighbors, it is unlikely that any of the committees will move in this direction— away from carrots and toward sticks—any time soon. However, a global body freed from the consensus constraint could be equipped and willing to set standards and hold states to them, going far beyond what the CTC or any entity subject to the UN's political and institutional limitations could achieve. A new global body could adopt a succinct set of standards and could have many more corrective tools available to it, such as "naming and shaming," to implement those standards. Freed from the consensus constraint, it might also exhibit a greater willingness to make use of such measures—something that the United States would likely find appealing.

In addition to these "corrective" measures, in order to enhance the likelihood of obtaining U.S. support, a global body would probably need to have some ability to refer or report noncompliant states to the Security Council. The attempts to use the IAEA's Security Council referral powers in the case of North Korea in the 1990s and Iran today have shown that this works much better on paper than in practice; the bulk of the international community is much less confrontational absent imminent violence than the United States tends to be. Nevertheless, the United States (as well as the other five permanent council members) is unlikely to give up the option, which currently exists only in theory, of having the Security Council impose Chapter VII enforcement measures against noncompliant states.

OVERCOMING SKEPTICISM IN THE UNITED STATES

Unfortunately, the growing recognition of the importance of deepening U.S. multilateral engagement in the fight against terrorism is coming at a time when Americans' support for the UN and enthusiasm for enhancing U.S.–UN cooperation is waning. The Oil-for-Food scandal, the Volcker Committee's findings, various congressional investigations, and the glacial pace of UN reform have led the U.S. public to grow increasingly disenchanted with the UN and, absent significant reforms, less likely to support giving it a leading role in addressing the most pressing global security problems.

According to a recently released Pew–Council on Foreign Relations survey, only about half of Americans (48 percent) now express a positive opinion of the UN, down from 77 percent in 2001.[21] In addition, this survey found that support for full cooperation with the UN has dropped from 67 percent three years ago to 54 percent today, with the steepest drop among groups that had been some of the UN's strongest supporters. This is the lowest it has been in almost thirty years. Finally, the importance Americans attach to the UN has also slipped, with only 40 percent of those surveyed saying that a stronger UN should be a top long-range U.S. priority.[22]

Since September 11, 2001, the U.S. government has envisioned only limited responsibility for the UN in the global fight against terrorism. This view on what the UN should contribute and is capable of contributing in this area is shared by many governments around the globe.[23] In short, neither the United States nor its allies would want the UN to assume a more robust counterterrorism role. Even if this were not the case, the UN's institutional and political limitations make it unsuited for playing such a role. Thus, having the UN continue to struggle to lead in the fight against terrorism, particularly in light of the declining support among Americans for the UN, is not a recipe for deepening U.S. engagement in multilateral counterterrorism efforts.

A new global body, freed from the constraints and history of the UN, and with the flexibility and expertise to make a difference on the ground, however, would be more likely to receive the support of U.S. elites. International organizations and bodies devoted to a specific issue—for example, atomic energy (IAEA), chemical weapons (OPCW), health (WHO), financing and development (IMF, World

Bank, UNDP), children (UNICEF), refugees (UNHCR)—generally receive high marks in the United States (particularly when compared to the UN's principal organs: the General Assembly, ECOSOC, the Security Council, the International Court of Justice, and the Secretariat), both within and outside government circles.[24] Thus, creating a specialized global counterterrorism body may increase the appetite for channeling more nonmilitary counterterrorism tasks through multilateral organizations.

A new body, sufficiently removed from the center of an ongoing debate about the effectiveness of the UN, would provide a forum for the United States to show its commitment to multilateral approaches to combating terrorism and enable it to work better with traditional and nontraditional allies in this area. In doing so, the United States would lend greater legitimacy to its counterterrorism efforts. Moreover, if the United States took a lead role in establishing a new body, it would go a long way to reassuring other countries that it sees terrorism as a truly global problem and is committed, where possible, to tackle the challenges it poses through peaceful, multilateral cooperation.

Of course, the devil is in the details, because the degree to which the United States would support the creation of a global counterterrorism body will ultimately depend on its specific features, its size, structure, budget, mandate, and effectiveness. Thus, careful consideration needs to be given to each of these issues before one embarks on a process of designing such a body.

EUROPE AND OTHER DEVELOPED STATES

Other developed countries such as the members of the European Union and the G8 as well as Norway and Australia would likely support a global counterterrorism body for many of the same reasons that the United States would do so. There is broad recognition among these and other countries that the current UN Security Council–led approach is not up to the task of coordinating the global counterterrorism capacity-building and monitoring effort. The July 2006 G8 leaders statement on strengthening the UN's counterterrorism program could be interpreted as criticism of the UN effort to date and the expression of a desire to see a more effective institutional mechanism for coordinating global, nonmilitary counterterrorism efforts.[25] A properly designed, dedicated global body could help ensure greater cohesion in worldwide efforts to prevent future attacks on their populations and assets at home and abroad.

After the March 2004 terrorist attacks in Madrid, European Union leaders declared, "The threat of terrorism is a threat to our security, our democracies, and our way of life in the European Union. We will do everything in our power to protect our people from this threat."[26] The EU Commission has acted on its own concerns related to lack of information sharing by proposing a number of ways to improve counterterrorism operational coordination and cooperation at the EU level as well as in countries in need of assistance outside the EU. The EU has made important strides in ensuring that its own members from the former Soviet bloc are capable of sharing information and enforcing counterterrorism measures. An effective global body could help ease technical assistance burdens on the major counterterrorism donors and provide them with help in analyzing and prioritizing countries' counterterrorism capacity needs. In addition, because a global body could include a technical assistance trust fund and the ability to provide assistance or training, it would allow donors that have funds but may lack trainers or expertise (for example, Denmark) to contribute more easily to global capacity-building efforts.

A dedicated global body could allow more states to play an active policymaking role than the current Security Council–led efforts afford. Its governing body would likely be significantly larger than the fifteen-member council and could include seats for the major counterterrorism donors. Thus, countries such as Germany, Japan, Italy, Spain, Australia, and Denmark could find themselves with permanent seats on the governing board. It is conceivable as well that the EU Commission, which participates in the G8, could find itself sitting around the new organization's policymaking table. Under the current approach, apart from the five permanent Security Council members, other countries, even the most active in the counterterrorism assistance field, will only rotate onto the Security Council and its subsidiary bodies every five to fifty years. Accordingly, they could be much more involved in setting the policies of the new organization than they are currently in the development of, for example, the CTC's policies. Moreover, the European countries that continue, with limited success, to push the UN Security Council bodies to pay more attention to human rights issues would be able to ensure these are adequately addressed during the negotiations of the mandate of the new body.

Finally, the current UN-led counterterrorism arrangement has failed to lead to a sustained U.S. commitment to using multilateral institutions to address the terrorist threat. By contrast, the United States has remained engaged in support of IAEA safeguards and other multilateral security initiatives to prevent proliferation. If designed properly, a global counterterrorism body could deepen the United States's engagement in multilateral counterterrorism efforts. This would likely be welcomed in many European and other national capitals.

9.

WHY GLOBAL SOUTH COUNTRIES COULD SUPPORT A GLOBAL COUNTERTERRORISM ORGANIZATION

For any global body to succeed and sustain the active interest of the wider international community over the long run, it needs vigorous participation from all points of the compass. Regarding terrorism specifically, the case for active multiregional participation is obvious and compelling. The global North and South both have a stake in preventing terrorism. Both developed and developing nations have suffered as a result of such attacks, and both must be represented as stakeholders in a new body for the enterprise to be effective.

The new body can play an important role in assessing the threat of terrorism at the local, regional, and global levels. The situation in Kenya highlights the importance of this issue. Two attacks have been perpetrated there in recent years, one in Nairobi in 1998 and another in Mombassa in 2002. The latter was perpetrated by local terror cells that allegedly had been captured after the first attack.[1] However, despite these horrific attacks and the loss of hundreds of their fellow citizens, Kenyans remain inclined to look at terrorism as a Western problem. They agree that it can have a profound effect on tourism, but it is not as pressing a concern as are HIV/AIDS and violent street crime.[2]

The perception that the United States is taking the threat seriously since September 11, 2001, but had little concern about foreign attacks before that date, is fairly widespread elsewhere in the world, particularly among the Group of 77 (G77) developing countries.[3] There is a sense among some Asian scholars, for example, that after September 11 the "perceived threat of terrorism" rather than the occurrence of terrorist attacks has created a new climate of fear.[4] The opportunity to exchange technical data on threat analysis would help to encourage a more cohesive approach to the problem of terrorism by addressing shared concerns. Any given state and the region in which it is situated could learn from the practices of others and add those lessons to their own cultural and regional experiences.

As described in chapter 3, from the viewpoint of many countries of the global South and perhaps beyond, the current UN Security Council–led arrangement has a number of flaws that have led to diminishing levels of cooperation. These include: (1) a proliferation of counterterrorism bodies with overlapping mandates and an increasing lack of coordination and cooperation among them; (2) the UN counterterrorism program being conceived of and overseen by the supposedly underrepresentative Security Council (and its subsidiary bodies), without much consultation with the wider UN membership; and (3) the requirement of a seemingly endless cycle of reporting without the Council's counterterrorism bodies being able to provide meaningful on-the-ground results, whether these be technical assistance or even simply a clear understanding of when or how the reporting process will be completed. Much of the global South not only feels excluded from the UN's counterterrorism policymaking and evaluation process, but finds itself getting nothing tangible in exchange for its cooperation.

Since September 11, 2001, the UN, through the Security Council, has demanded that states take a series of steps to improve their capacities to fight terrorism. However, it has been unable to identify clear priorities for each country and then deliver or even facilitate delivery of the assistance and resources needed to address them. In short, countries of the South increasingly view the UN-led response to global terrorism as inadequate. Because effectively countering the global threat of terrorism requires a broadly cooperative effort involving countries of the global North and South, this dwindling support for the UN program from the latter signals trouble.

PROPOSALS FROM THE SOUTH

The growing dissatisfaction among many countries of the global South with current UN counterterrorism efforts has led several states to offer proposals on how to improve the UN's performance in this area and the global multilateral counterterrorism effort more generally. For example, in fall 2004, the Costa Rican ambassador to the UN not only pointed out the problems with the current approach but offered a solution:

> The [UN's] contribution to fighting terrorism needs to encompass all existing UN efforts in order to be effective. In the era of its revitalization, the United Nations has to seriously address the issues of our time, maximizing the use of its limited resources. Overlapping, repeating, improvising, competing efforts are a luxury we cannot afford. . . .
>
> Since all of us and all of our peoples are actual or potential victims of terrorism, all Member States must be involved in developing and establishing the Organization's counterterrorism policies. . . . The fight against terrorism and its root causes must become a permanent and routine activity of the United Nations and of the General Assembly.
>
> For this reason, the Government of Costa Rica is suggesting that the General Assembly should begin an in-depth review of the various United Nations mandates and bodies dealing with terrorism, with the aim of eliminating duplication, unifying resources and centralizing decision-making in the hands of a professional, permanent, and impartial body located at the centre of the Organization. This is the rationale behind our proposal of the establishment of a United Nations High Commissioner on Terrorism.
>
> This year, the General Assembly should request the Secretary-General to present to it . . . a report considering possible methods, mandate, and structure of the Office of the High Commissioner on Terrorism.
>
> Next year, the General Assembly should establish an open-ended working group to determine the mandate and structure of that new institution.[5]

A year later, the General Assembly had not acted on this proposal, although it did request the secretary-general to submit proposals to strengthen the capacity of the UN system to assist states in combating terrorism and enhance coordination of UN activities in this regard.[6] Subsequent to making this proposal, the Costa Ricans indicated that the UN high commissioner idea was simply one possible way of fixing the problems of too many different committees, lack of coordination, and overlapping mandates.[7]

Other states of the global South also have proposed ways to address these problems. For example, in February 2005 the government of Saudi Arabia convened an international counterterrorism conference of more than fifty countries as well as international and regional organizations. At the meeting, the crown prince proposed the establishment of an international counterterrorism center "under the auspices of the UN" to, among other things, "develop a mechanism for exchanging information and expertise between States," encourage the establishment of national and regional centers, and provide assistance to developing countries to deal with crises and terrorist acts.[8] The proposal, which was also put forward by the Saudi foreign minister and endorsed by the fifty-five-member OIC during the sixtieth UN General Assembly, has not found much support with countries in the global North and has thus stalled at the UN.[9] In late November 2005, however, the Saudis convinced the interior ministers of the five other Gulf Cooperation Council (GCC) states (Bahrain, Kuwait, Oman, Qatar, and the United Arab Emirates) "to take action on a regional level by approving a special panel to combat terrorism."[10] Although it is unclear just what type of structure the GCC has in mind, if the establishment of such a panel will strengthen coordination of counterterrorism efforts in that region, it may have a lasting and positive impact in a region that is notably weak in the field of counterterrorism compared to Europe or North America. It also remains to be seen whether the GCC will seek support for expanding the panel beyond the regional to the global level.

The limitations of the Saudi proposal for an international counterterrorism center are neither in its analysis of the current problems facing the international community nor in the call for a more coordinated and sufficiently funded effort to address those problems. Rather, support is constrained by the fact that the proposal is sponsored by a state that naturally has its own political agenda, is seen by some to have a mixed record in combating jihadist terrorism, and has complex historical relations with other states. In addition, although Saudi Arabia recommends that the center "should be established under the principles of the UN and its relevant resolutions and committees," it offers no guidance on how this might be done.

The Pakistani ambassador to the UN recently urged the Security Council:

to evolve a mechanism to associate the larger Membership of the United Nations with the Council's work, especially in the field of terrorism, since global cooperation is so essential in that field. It could be done, for example, by opening the Membership of the counter-terrorism committees to other United Nations Member States through elections. The ultimate decision making would of course rest with the Security Council. That would promote inclusiveness, provide alternative perspectives and views and enhance transparency and accountability in the work of the three committees.[11]

During the subsequent discussions surrounding the elaboration of a General Assembly counterterrorism strategy, he has voiced support for the Saudi proposal, arguing for an institutional arrangement "that is universally accepted, governed, and supervised by the General Assembly, thus involving all Member States."[12]

In addition, the Egyptian foreign minister, in an October 2005 letter to the UN secretary-general, "proposed the convening of a special session of the General Assembly to examine and adopt a UN action plan for cooperation against terrorism."[13] This proposal received the support of nearly all fifty-five members of the OIC when it was discussed in fall 2005. Among other things, it is aimed at the development of a new UN framework for coordinating the various UN counterterrorism activities, moving beyond the "limited" Security Council–led approach.[14]

Each of these proposals appears aimed at addressing some of the problems identified with the current UN approach. If adopted, however, none would be likely to address enough of the problems to make a significant difference in terms of the UN's ability to contribute to the global counterterrorism effort. As long as the UN's counterterrorism programs remain part of one or more of the UN's principal organs and thus subject to their political and institutional constraints, a reorganization or consolidation of the existing programs or the establishment of new ones will not produce the kind of substantive results that many countries of the global South are seeking.

In addition, the kind of innovative thinking that is needed to design a multilateral counterterrorism body capable of spearheading global, nonmilitary efforts is unlikely to come from the secretary-general, as competing political and institutional interests would likely inhibit his ability to put forward the type of creative proposal that is needed to make a difference on the ground. This dynamic within the UN seriously diminishes the likelihood that the secretary-general's recently established Counter-Terrorism Implementation Task Force, which includes representatives of the different offices within the UN system that are engaged in counterterrorism activity, will do more than discuss mandates and ways to improve cooperation among the different UN offices. In fact, while the first product of the task force's efforts, the secretary-general's "recommendations for a global counterterrorism strategy" does put forward a number of pragmatic and useful proposals in these areas, it falls short of the more far-reaching ones that are needed to make a real difference.

THE CASE FOR SOUTHERN SUPPORT

Proposals such as the Costa Rican, Saudi, and Pakistani ones outlined earlier indicate that there appears to be an appetite among many countries of the global South (and beyond) for considering ways to improve multilateral counterterrorism capacity-building efforts. There are compelling reasons why many developing countries might be inclined to support the establishment of a global body dedicated to coordinating those efforts over a simple reshuffling of the current UN arrangement.

First, developing countries could participate in the process that designs the structure and establishes the mandate of this new body, something they were excluded from when the Security Council began to act. Second, as with EU members and other developed states, they would have greater representation on the organization's governing body, which could be considerably larger than the fifteen-member Security Council. Thus, they would be much more involved in setting the policies of the organization than is currently the case with the development of, for example, the CTC's policies. Third, another limitation of the current UN-led approach has been its inability to promote the cross-fertilization of best practices from one region to another. A global body with the capacity to promote and disseminate best practices would enable other regions to benefit from the experience and expertise of bodies as diverse as the EU, G8, and APEC. Fourth, as with states in the developing world, the global South would welcome the deeper U.S. multilateral engagement on counterterrorism that would result from the creation of an effective, and properly resourced, dedicated body.

Fifth, such a body could be removed from the political and institutional limitations of the UN's principal organs and thus operate more effectively and efficiently, focusing less on paper and more on results. Because the same group of countries would be involved in setting the budget, mandates, and policies of the new body, unlike the current UN Security Council–led approach, it would also be more likely to have the necessary human and financial resources and technical expertise to allow it to fulfill the global capacity-building and coordinating functions that the CTC is supposed to be filling. With a new global body that coordinates better with donors, states would have their technical assistance needs identified and filled more quickly in a manner that helps to ensure that multilateral counterterrorism measures are implemented effectively and in a manner that reinforces development and good governance. This would benefit assistance recipients in developing countries as well as donors, including the United States and other G8 countries, who have been frustrated by the CTC's poor track record on coherently identifying assistance needs. In addition, an adequately resourced and staffed global counterterrorism body could provide a much-needed boost to those regional and subregional organizations in the global South that lack the financial and/or political support to develop a meaningful counterterrorism program. The UN Security Council's CTC was supposed to help address this gap, but for the reasons described in chapter 3 has had little success in doing so.

Sixth, a broad-based counterterrorism organization that effectively coordinates global technical assistance would reinforce good governance and enhance development. Creating more effective law enforcement capabilities, including through the training of judges, prosecutors, intelligence officials, and police; improving border, immigration, and customs controls; regulating banks and financial institutions; and strengthening security at ports and border crossings will do much more than simply improve counterterrorism capacity. These improvements would parallel the steps increasingly recognized among aid donors and recipients as essential to economic development and the expansion of social and economic opportunity. Trade and investment depend on stable government and the rule of law. Many counterterrorism technical assistance measures improve governance capacity more generally and thus also advance the prospects for economic development. In fact, although counterterrorism activities are traditionally viewed very differently by the security and development communities (the former tends to be mainly concerned with enforcement and protection while the latter has a focus on more fundamental structural issues), the two are interdependent. The close relationship between security and development is increasingly acknowledged as donors have realized that development, understood as poverty reduction, can only be obtained and sustained if institutions and mechanisms of governance ensure the security and safety of citizens.[15] Hence the question of good governance—the optimum functioning of these institutions—has received increased attention from the development community. Meanwhile, international security actors have also realized that short-term operations related to counterterrorism or another issue of concern to the international community will not bring sustainable benefit without attention to underlying longer-term development work. Attention to this linkage, with focus on technical measures such as improving judicial competences, can improve counterterrorism mandates and broader governance goals. An approach that enacts measures addressing a broader range of concerns can help to reduce the stigma of security-related demands placed on the developing world and would encourage more participation.

This linkage between technical assistance and development suggests the need for integrated development aid strategies that include a global nonmilitary counterterrorism program. The UNDP may have a role to play in this regard as well. Linking the increased international commitment to counterterrorism capacity building to the broader development agenda would enable assistance providers and development officials to work together in combating terrorism and promoting development. Thus, the process of establishing an international body that is capable of facilitating technical assistance would build much more global support if it ensures that the legitimacy of development objectives is not threatened but rather reinforced.[16]

Finally, a dedicated global counterterrorism body would provide states with another alternative to working bilaterally with the United States on counterterrorism capacity-building issues, something that has been a difficulty for some states in the current political climate. For example, the United States and Syria, who have been able to cooperate in discrete instances during the global war on terrorism despite an otherwise strained relationship, could expand their cooperation against terrorism under the aegis of an effective global counterterrorism body.

Although it is likely that a dedicated counterterrorism body could be created with the support of the global South, the degree of this support will depend on the process for creating it, as well as its structure, mandate, and relationship to the UN. As with the question of whether the United States would support the establishment of a global body, the answer is probably yes, with the devil being in the details. While the members of the global South have expressed an interest in improving the effectiveness of the UN counterterrorism program and offered proposals for structural change, their support will diminish the more such change moves in the direction of a new institution focused on setting standards, grading performance, and identifying nonperformers, as opposed to identifying and filling capacity needs. Meanwhile, the United States and some of its key partners in the fight against terrorism may be less inclined to support a new institution that lacks these capabilities. In the end, the challenge will be to design a body that can address the concerns and satisfy the needs of both the United States (and its Northern partners) and countries of the global South, resolving the trade-offs between the two.

10.

AN INTERNATIONAL PROCESS ON THE CREATION OF A GLOBAL COUNTERTERRORISM BODY

This book has highlighted the limitations of the current, diffuse, Security Council–led, multilateral, nonmilitary counterterrorism effort. It has noted that, in the near-term, even a more consolidated, coherent council program would not be able to meet the challenges posed by the evolving global terrorist threat. It has concluded that a more coordinated and effective multilateral initiative, freed from the political and institutional limitations of the UN, is needed. Although it has argued that a global, stand-alone body may be needed to coordinate multilateral, nonmilitary counterterrorism efforts and meet the serious external challenges posed by constantly adapting terrorist networks, there may be other ameliorative steps that could be taken as well at the global, regional, and/or subregional levels. For example, regional and subregional counterterrorism mechanisms could be strengthened and coordination among them improved. As this book highlights, many of the high-threat regions of the world lack an effective counterterrorism body (or even program) capable of working with countries in the region to implement counterterrorism mandates or engaging in any meaningful way with the UN or functional organizations such as ICAO or the IMO.

Accordingly, serious consideration should be given to examining ways to improve the current nonmilitary counterterrorism effort at all levels, which should include the possibility of establishing a global body devoted to counterterrorism.

To guarantee that this issue is studied and discussed among a broad array of technical experts and political stakeholders in the global North and South, a broad-based international process should be developed. Such a process could include a series of workshops and meetings in different regions to bring together counterterrorism experts and relevant policymakers offering diverse cultural perspectives to further explore the issue areas outlined in this book. This process could include an examination of the models outlined in chapter 7 and the creation of a blueprint for a technical, intergovernmental organization, staffed by independent experts, to simultaneously enhance and depoliticize multilateral counterterrorism efforts. Subjects related to particular regions and discrete technical and legal issues should be covered by experts with backgrounds and experience in those areas to account for cultural practices and to foster sufficiently detailed expert input.

The goal of the process should be to develop a succinct set of policy recommendations outlining concrete steps to be taken to improve the global, nonmilitary counterterrorism effort, which might include, but not be limited to, the establishment of an international counterterrorism body. Project partners would then need to produce a comprehensive report (possibly with interim reports on some of the discrete issues) to inform policymakers and experts. The process should culminate with policy briefings in New York for members of the UN community, including both member state and UN Secretariat officials, and for the officials of interested governments in various capitals.

APPENDIXES

APPENDIX 1. THE UNITED NATIONS SYSTEM AND COUNTERTERRORISM: THE MAIN ACTORS

RELEVANT PRINCIPAL UNITED NATIONS ORGANS

Economic and Social Council		General Assembly	Secretariat
United Nations Commission on Crime Prevention and Criminal Justice		Sixth Committee	1566 Working Group UNSCR 1566 (2004)
United Nations Office on Drugs and Crime		Terrorism Ad Hoc Committee	

Security Council

Al-Qaida and Taliban Sanctions Committee UNSCR 1267 (1999)

Counter-Terrorism Committee UNSCR 1373 (2001)

1540 Committee UNSCR 1540 (2004)

Staff Bodies

The Analytical Support and Sanctions Monitoring Team UNSCR 1526 (2004)

Counter-Terrorism Executive Directorate UNSCR 1535 (2004)

1540 Committee Group of Experts UNSCR 1540 (2004)

APPENDIX 2. EXAMPLES OF ORGANIZATIONAL MODELS

ORGANIZATION	MANDATE	FOUNDING DOCUMENT(S)	MEMBERSHIP	SIZE OF SECRETARIAT	SIZE/COMPOSITION OF GOVERNING BODY	FUNDING MECHANISM AND BUDGET	DECISIONMAKING PROCESS/COMPLIANCE
TREATY-BASED ORGANIZATIONS							
International Atomic Energy Agency (IAEA)	Promotes the peaceful use of atomic energy while ensuring nuclear cooperation does not contribute to the proliferation of nuclear weapons	Statute of the IAEA (1956)	138 member states	2,244 staff (roughly half professional and half support staff)	The General Conference is composed of representatives from all of the IAEA's 138 member states. The Board of Governors has 35 members, of which 13 are designated by the board (includes the 10 members most advanced in the technology of atomic energy and the member most advanced in each of 7 regional groups) and 22 are elected by the General Conference (based largely on equitable geographic representation). Both the General Conference and Board of Governors approve and guide the work of the Secretariat.	The IAEA's 2004 regular budget was $268.5 million from IAEA-agreed assessments, plus a target of $75 million in voluntary contributions. An additional $55 million was received in 2004 in extra-budgetary funds.	According to the IAEA statute, in both the General Conference and the board, important decisions such as those relating to the budget, appointment of the Director General, and compliance are taken by a two-thirds majority while other decisions are taken by a simple majority vote. IAEA inspectors report noncompliance with IAEA safeguards to the Director General who refers reports of noncompliance to the Board of Governors. If the board determines a state to be in noncompliance, it is required to report that state to the UN Security Council and General Assembly for appropriate action. The IAEA Board may suspend assistance, revoke previously provided assistance and materials, and suspend a noncompliant state's membership.

Organization	Purpose	Legal basis	Membership	Staff	Governance	Budget	Notes
International Civil Aviation Organization (ICAO)	Sets international standards and recommended practices for civil aviation and offers technical assistance to enhance aviation safety and security	Convention on International Civil Aviation (Chicago Convention, 1944)	188 member states	268 professional staff	The assembly is composed of representatives of all the member states and meets at least once every three years to review the work of ICAO and give guidance for future work. The council, which guides ICAO's work, consists of 36 member states elected by the assembly, giving adequate representation to states of chief importance in air transport, states which make the largest contribution to the provision of facilities for international civil air navigation; states from all major geographic areas are represented.	ICAO's 2004 regular budget was $54.5 million from ICAO-agreed assessments. Assessments are based on a country's economic factors and relative importance in civil aviation with a maximum assessment of 25 percent.	According to the Chicago Convention, unless otherwise decided, both the assembly and council take decisions by a majority vote. The council issues standards which require uniform application and to which members have agreed to conform unless they notify the council that it is impracticable to do so, and recommends practices members are expected "to endeavor to perform." The council reports to the assembly any infraction of the Chicago Convention, as well as any failure to carry out recommendations or determinations of the council.

Continued on next page

APPENDIX 2. EXAMPLES OF ORGANIZATIONAL MODELS (CONTINUED)

ORGANIZATION	MANDATE	FOUNDING DOCUMENT(S)	MEMBERSHIP	SIZE OF SECRETARIAT	SIZE/COMPOSITION OF GOVERNING BODY	FUNDING MECHANISM AND BUDGET	DECISIONMAKING PROCESS/COMPLIANCE
International Organization for Migration (IOM)	Promotes humane and orderly migration worldwide by delivering advice and services to migrants and governments	Constitution of the International Organization for Migration (1951)	116 member states	5,000 staff worldwide (225 at headquarters in Geneva)	The council, the decisionmaking body, is composed of representatives of all the member states. The Executive Committee is composed of 16 representatives of the member states elected for two-year terms by the council.	IOM's 2004 budget was $637.8 million based on voluntary and assessed contributions from member states.	According to the IOM Constitution, some decisions require a two-thirds majority vote, but unless otherwise decided, most decisions of the council, the Executive Committee and all subcommittees are taken by a simple majority vote.
Interpol	Facilitates cross-border police cooperation and supports and assists all organizations, authorities, and services whose mission it is to combat crime	1923 ICPO Interpol Constitution	184 member states	450 staff (one-third are seconded or detached from national law enforcement agencies)	The General Assembly is composed of representatives of all the member states which meet once a year and take decisions affecting general policy and the resources needed for international cooperation, working methods, finances, and programs of activities. The Executive Committee is a 13-member body (elected based on achieving a certain degree of regional balance) that meets three times a year to, among other things, supervise the execution of the	Interpol's 2003 budget was 37 million euros based on a framework of statutory contributions agreed to by member states.	According to the ICPO-Interpol constitution, both the General Assembly and the Executive Committee, generally take decisions by a simple majority vote.

| World Health Organization (WHO) | UN specialized agency for health that seeks to provide the highest level of health attainable by all peoples through programming to mitigate world health issues while improving national standards of health | WHO Constitution (1948) | 192 member states | 4,000 professional and support staff (1,220 at headquarters in Geneva) | decisions of the General Assembly and the administration and work of the secretary-general. The World Health Assembly, the supreme policymaking body for the WHO, is composed of representatives of all the member states and elects the members of the Executive Board. The Executive Board consists of 32 technical experts elected by the assembly (taking into account equitable geographic distribution) and serving as government representatives, who give effect to the decisions and policies of the Assembly and generally advise and facilitate its work. | The WHO's 2004 regular budget was $430 million from contributions using the UN scale of assessments. | According to WHO Constitution, World Health Assembly and Executive Board decisions are taken by a two-thirds majority vote. |

Continued on next page

APPENDIX 2. EXAMPLES OF ORGANIZATIONAL MODELS (CONTINUED)

ORGANIZATION	MANDATE	FOUNDING DOCUMENT(S)	MEMBERSHIP	SIZE OF SECRETARIAT	SIZE/COMPOSITION OF GOVERNING BODY	FUNDING MECHANISM AND BUDGET	DECISIONMAKING PROCESS/COMPLIANCE
			INFORMAL, POLITICAL-BASED ARRANGEMENTS				
Australia Group	Multilateral export control regime established to limit the transfer of items that may contribute to the spread of biological, toxin, and chemical weapons	Australia Group Guidelines and Control lists	39 participating states	Australia's Department of Foreign Affairs and Trade functions as the informal chair and secretariat of the group, performing the administrative, coordinating, and convening functions	Annual plenary meetings of representatives from participating states	N/A—voluntary	Decisions are taken by consensus. As an informal, nonbinding arrangement, there is no formal mechanism to enforce compliance, but participants do periodically use intelligence and diplomatic pressure to identify and discourage transfers inconsistent with the regime's guidelines and control lists. Unlike the other multilateral export control regimes, the group does track implementation of agreed controls by participating states.
Egmont Group	An informal group that promotes international cooperation, best practices, and information sharing between Financial Intelligence Units (FIUs) to better combat money laundering, terrorist financing, and other financial crimes	The Egmont Definition of a Financial Intelligence Unit Statement of Purpose of the Egmont Group of Financial Intelligence Units	Over 100 countries with recognized operational FIU units meeting the Egmont Group's Definition	Nopermanent secretariat; administrative functions are shared on a rotating basis. The rotating Egmont Support Position, Working Groups, and the Egmont Committee are used to conduct common business.	Annual plenary meetings of representatives from member FIUs	N/A—voluntary contributions from member FIUs; more formalized funding mechanism(s) currently under consideration	Decisions are taken by consensus. The Egmont Group has outlined procedures to address those members that may no longer meet the established definitions and standards of the Egmont Group or fail to exchange information.

Financial Action Task Force (FATF)	Intergovernmental body that establishes international standards and best practices and develops, promotes, and monitors implementation of both national and international policies to combat money laundering and the financing of terrorism	FATF-agreed document; currently operating under eight-year mandate agreed to in 2004	33 members (31 member jurisdictions and the European Commission and the Gulf Co-operation Council)	10 staff; the FATF secretariat housed at the OEDC headquarters supports the work of the annual FATF meetings, the president, and steering group.	Annual plenary and working group meetings of representatives from members. FATF's steering group, an advisory body which sets the direction and priority of FATF's work. The presidency, a one-year rotating position held by a high-level government official from a member jurisdiction	FATF's 2004 budget was $1.636 million from assessed contributions by member jurisdictions based on the OECD scale of assessments, a formula based on the size of a jurisdiction's economy.	Decisions are taken by consensus. Although FATF is an informal, nonbinding arrangement, it has developed mechanisms to enforce compliance. Compliance/implementation of FATF standards and recommendations is measured through self-assessment and mutual evaluation processes. FATF maintains a list of non-cooperative countries and territories (NCCT) which are judged as such based on their overall regulatory framework, customer identification, suspicious transaction reporting, criminalization of money laundering, and level of international cooperation. Noncompliant jurisdictions may be subject to extra scrutiny and countermeasures by member jurisdictions and financial institutions.
Missile Technology Control Regime (MTCR)	Multilateral export control regime established to control transfers that could contribute to delivery systems (other than manned aircraft) for weapons of mass destruction	MTCR Guidelines (or common export control policy) and the MTCR Equipment, Software and Technology Annex (list of controlled items)	34 participating states	No secretariat; a permanent administrative point of contact (France) and rotating chair perform the logistical, outreach, and coordinating functions for the regime and its annual plenary meetings.	Annual plenary meetings of representatives from participating states	N/A—voluntary	Decisions are taken by consensus. As an informal, nonbinding arrangement, there is no formal mechanism to enforce compliance, but participants do periodically use intelligence and diplomatic pressure to identify and discourage transfers inconsistent with the regime's guidelines and control lists.

Continued on next page

APPENDIX 2. EXAMPLES OF ORGANIZATIONAL MODELS (CONTINUED)

ORGANIZATION	MANDATE	FOUNDING DOCUMENT(S)	MEMBERSHIP	SIZE OF SECRETARIAT	SIZE/COMPOSITION OF GOVERNING BODY	FUNDING MECHANISM AND BUDGET	DECISIONMAKING PROCESS/COMPLIANCE
Wassenaar Arrangement on Export Controls for Conventional Arms and Dual Use Goods and Technologies	Multilateral export control regime established to prevent "destabilizing" transfers of conventional arms and dual use goods and technologies	Initial Elements (1996)	39 participating states	13 staff (more than half of whom are specialized professionals)	Annual plenary meetings of representatives from participating states	The Wassenaar Arrangement's total 2003 budget was 1.375 million euros based on assessed contributions from participating states.	Decisions are taken by consensus. As an informal, non-binding arrangement, there is no formal mechanism to enforce compliance, but participants do periodically use intelligence and diplomatic pressure to identify and discourage transfers inconsistent with the regime's guidelines and control lists.
				UN PROGRAMS			
Joint United Nations Programme on HIV/AIDS (UNAIDS)	Works in countries dealing with the HIV/AIDS epidemic, primarily through coordination theme groups that seek to mobilize all sectors to address AIDS	ECOSOC resolution (1994/24) endorsed the establishment; 1996 Memorandum of Understanding by the six original cosponsoring UN bodies	N/A— UN Program	196 staff (147 professionals)	UNAIDS Program Coordinating Board (PCB) is the governing body for all programmatic issues concerning policy, strategy, finance, monitoring, and evaluation of UNAIDS. The PCB consists of 22 member states based on equitable regional distribution, nine cosponsoring organizations (with no right to vote), and five NGOs (with no right to vote or participate in the formal decisionmaking process).	UNAIDS's core voluntary budget for 2004 was $145.8 million plus an additional $4.7 million in extra-budgetary funds.	According to the modus operandi of the PCB, the board seeks to adopt decisions by consensus, but should voting be required, decisions are taken by majority vote.

| United Nations Development Programme (UNDP) | Promotes global development through development assistance programs that empower nations to find solutions to global and national development issues | UN General Assembly Resolution 2029 (XX) (1965) | N/A— UN Program | 5,800 staff (2,500 professionals) | The Executive Board, which oversees and supports UNDP's work and reports to the Economic and Social Council, is made up of 36 representatives elected on a rotating basis by the General Assembly to serve four-year terms with special consideration given to the provision of adequate regional representation. | UNDP's 2004 regular budget was $842 million, plus an additional $3 billion in voluntary contributions. | According to the UNDP rules of procedure, Executive Board decisions are taken by majority votes but the practice is to take decisions by consensus. |
| United Nations Environmental Programme (UNEP) | Provides leadership and encourages partnership in caring for the environment by inspiring, informing, and promoting development without compromising the environment | UN General Assembly Resolution 2997 (XXVII) (1972) | N/A— UN Program | 487 professionals in the UNEP Executive Directorate | UNEP's Governing Council is composed of 58 members elected to four-year terms by the UN General Assembly taking into account the principle of equitable regional representation. The Governing Council reports to the UN General Assembly through the Economic and Social Council. Committee of Permanent Representatives | UNEP's 2004 budget was $130 million; about 4 percent from the UN regular budget, the remainder from voluntary contributions through various trust funds, the Environmental Fund, and partnerships with individual member states. | According to UNEP rules of procedure, except where expressly provided, decisions of the Governing Council are taken by a majority of the members present and voting but the practice is to take decisions by consensus. |

Continued on next page

APPENDIX 2. EXAMPLES OF ORGANIZATIONAL MODELS (CONTINUED)

ORGANIZATION	MANDATE	FOUNDING DOCUMENT(S)	MEMBERSHIP	SIZE OF SECRETARIAT	SIZE/COMPOSITION OF GOVERNING BODY	FUNDING MECHANISM AND BUDGET	DECISIONMAKING PROCESS/COMPLIANCE
United Nations High Commissioner for Refugees (UNHCR)	Provides international protection to refugees and other persons of concern and seeks to find durable solutions to their plight and furnish them with material assistance.	Statute of the Office of the UN High Commissioner for Refugees was embodied in General Assembly Resolution 428(V) (1950). Executive Committee established by ECOSOC resolution 672/XXV (1958)	N/A— UN Program	6,000 staff	The Executive Committee meets once a year and consists of 66 members, elected on the widest possible geographic basis from those states (UN members and others) with a demonstrated interest in, and devotion to, the solution of refugee problems; approves budget and provides policy guidance to UNHCR; and reports directly to the UN General Assembly.	UNHCR's 2004 budget consisted of $28 million from the UN regular budget plus around $1 billion in voluntary contributions.	According to its rules of procedure, Executive Committee chairman generally "ascertain(s) the sense of the meeting in lieu of a formal vote." If the chairman proceeds to a vote, then majority rules.
Office of the United Nations High Commissioner for Human Rights (OHCHR)	The High Commissioner is the principal UN official for advancing UN human rights activities. The OHCHR works to ensure practical implementation of universally recognized human rights norms by carrying out the tasks assigned by UN human rights bodies.	General Assembly Resolution 48/141 (1993)	N/A— UN Program	576 staff (304 at headquarters in Geneva)	No governing body, as such; OHCHR acts under the direction and authority of the secretary-general and within the framework of the overall competence, authority, and decisions of the General Assembly, the Economic and Social Council, and the Commission on Human Rights.	The OHCHR's 2005 budget was about $90 million of which $30 million came from the UN regular budget and the rest from voluntary contributions.	N/A

NOTES

CHAPTER 1

1. May 26, 2006, speech at Georgetown University, available at http://www.britainusa.com/sections/articles_show_nt1.asp?a=41943&i=4102 9&L1=41004&L2=41029&d=-1.

2. In various audio and video tapes, al Qaeda has warned of additional attacks against the United States. In an audio tape dated December 2005, Osama bin Laden warned of additional terrorist attacks in the United States, indicating, "The operations are under preparation and you will see them in your homes the minute they are through, with God's permission." As quoted in Hassan M. Fattah, "Bin Laden Re-emerges, Warning U.S. While Offering 'Truce,'" *New York Times*, January 19, 2006. Intelligence analysts, academics, and policy makers also warn of another large-scale terrorist attack against the United States. See, for example: Daniel Benjamin and Steven Simon, *The Next Attack: The Failure of the War on Terror and a Strategy for Getting It Right* (New York: Times Books, 2005).

3. Former U.S. secretary of defense William Perry, Graham Allison of the John F. Kennedy School of Government, and others have warned that, given the current state of affairs, unless aggressive preventive measures are taken there is a greater than 50 percent chance of a nuclear terrorist attack before the end of the decade. Graham Allison, "How to Stop Nuclear Terror," *Foreign Affairs* 83, no. 1 (2004). William Perry, "Keynote Address to Post-Cold War U.S. Nuclear Strategy: A Search for Technical and Policy Common Ground," National Academy of Sciences, Washington, D.C., August 11, 2004.

4. Matthew Bun, John P. Holdren, and Anthony Wier, "Securing Nuclear Weapons and Materials: Seven Steps for Immediate Action," Managing the Atom project, Belfer Center for Science and International Affairs, John F. Kennedy School of Government, May 2002.

5. Lowell E. Jacoby, "Statement for the Record before the Senate Select Committee on Intelligence," February 16, 2005.

6. Rahimullah Yusufzai, "Conversation with Terror," *Time,* January 11, 1999.

7. Anthony Cordesman, "The Lessons of International Cooperation in Counterterrorism," address to the RUSI Conference on Transnational Terrorism "A Global Approach," January 18, 2006.

8. Numerous leaders have made this point, including Kofi Annan, who has noted that "terrorism is a threat to all States, to all people, which can strike anytime, anywhere." Secretary-General's Global Strategy for Fighting Terrorism, March 11, 2005, http://www.un.org/News/Press/docs/2005 /sgsm9757.doc.htm, accessed December 15, 2005; and U.S. President George W. Bush has remarked, "The global threat of terrorism requires a global response." The White House, "President Bush Discusses Progress in the War on Terror," Oak Ridge National Laboratory, Oak Ridge, Tennessee, July 12, 2004.

9. The White House Office of the Press Secretary, "Joint Statement on Counterterrorism Cooperation: Joint Statement by President George W. Bush and President Vladimir V. Putin on Counterterrorism Cooperation," Washington, D.C., May 24, 2002.

10. William P. Pope, "European Cooperation with the United States in the Global War on Terrorism," remarks to the House International Relations Committee, Subcommittee on Europe and on International Terrorism, Nonproliferation and Human Rights, Washington, D.C., September 14, 2004.

11. International Crisis Group, "Counter-Terrorism in Somalia: Losing Hearts and Minds?" *Africa Report,* no. 95, July 11, 2005.

12. "Nations Cup Bomb Plot Foiled by SA Spooks," *Cape Times,* February 13, 2006,http://www.int.iol.co.za/index.php?set_id=1&click_id=85&art_id =vn20060213034520520C323662, accessed June 4, 2006.

13. The 9/11 Commission's report recommended, among other things, "The United States has the resources and the people. The government should combine them more effectively, achieving unity of effort. We offer five major recommendations to do that: Unifying strategic intelligence and operational planning against Islamic terrorists across the foreign-domestic divide with a National Counterterrorism Center; Unifying the intelligence community with a new National Intelligence Director; Unifying the many participants in the counterterrorism effort and their knowledge in network-based information-sharing systems that transcend traditional governmental boundaries; Unifying and strengthening congressional oversight to improve quality and accountability; and Strengthening the FBI and homeland defenders." National Commission on Terrorist Attacks upon the United States, *The 9/11 Commission Report: Final Report of the National Commission on Terrorist Attacks Upon the United States ("9/11 Commission Report")* (Washington, D.C.: U.S. Government Printing Office, 2004), pp. 399–400.

14. For example, the CTC was created immediately following the September 11 terrorist attacks in the United States; in 2004, the discovery of A. Q. Kahn's clandestine nuclear trafficking network and a massacre at a school seized by armed Chechen militants in the Russian town of Beslan led to resolutions establishing additional Security Council counterterrorism-related bodies.

CHAPTER 2

1. *American Interests on UN Reform: Report of the Task Force on the United Nations* (Washington, D.C.: United States Institute of Peace, 2005), p. 76.

2. In addition to the General Assembly and Security Council and its subsidiary bodies, the other parts of the UN involved in counterterrorism-related issues include: the Department of Peacekeeping Operations, the Department of Political Affairs, the Department of Public Information, the Department for Disarmament Affairs, the Department of Safety and Security, the International Atomic Energy Agency, the International Civil Aviation Organization, the International Maritime Organization, Interpol, the Office on Drugs and Crime, the Office of the High Commissioner for Human Rights, the Office of Legal Affairs, the Organisation for the Prohibition of Chemical Weapons, United Nations Development Programme, United Nations Educational, Scientific and Cultural Organization, the World Customs Organization, the World Health Organization, the Special Rapporteur on the Promotion and Protection of Human Rights While Countering Terrorism, and the three Security Council staff bodies: the Counter-Terrorism Committee Executive Directorate, the Al-Qaida and Taliban Sanctions Committee Analytical Support and Sanctions Monitoring Team, and the 1540 Committee's Group of Experts.

3. Robert Alden, "Waldheim Bids U.N. Acts on Terrorism," *New York Times*, September 13, 1972.

4. Ibid.

5. The Convention on Offences and Certain Other Acts Committed on Board Aircraft (Tokyo) (1963), the Convention for the Suppression of Unlawful Seizure of Aircraft (Hague) (1970), and Convention for the Suppression of Unlawful Acts Against the Safety of Civil Aviation (1971).

6. Convention on the Prevention and Punishment of Crimes Against Internationally Protected Persons (New York) (1973) and International Convention Against the Taking of Hostages (New York) (1979).

7. See, for example, United Nations General Assembly Resolution 3166 (XXVIII), December 14, 1973, and United Nations General Assembly Resolution 34/146, December 17, 1979.

8. Kendall W. Stiles, "The Power of Procedure and the Procedures of the Powerful: Anti-Terror Law in the United Nations," *Journal of Peace Research* 43, no. 1 (January 2006): 42.

9. Declaration on Measures to Eliminate International Terrorism, United Nations General Assembly Resolution 49/60, December 9, 1994, para. 3.

10. Convention on Combating International Terrorism, Organisation of Islamic Conferences (1999), Article 2(a).

11. OAU Convention on the Prevention and Combating of Terrorism, July 14, 1999, Article 3.

12. For example, the sanctions the council imposed against Libya in 1992 for its role in the bombing of Pan Am flight no. 103 (and UTA flight no. 772) were the first for terrorist acts under Chapter VII of the UN Charter and, in the view of some, contributed to getting Libya to cease its support of terrorism. See United Nations Security Council Resolution S/RES/731, January 21, 1992; Thomas E. McNamara, "Survival Instinct: Why Qaddafi Turned His Back on Terror," *International Herald Tribune,* May 5, 2004.

13. United Nations Security Council Resolution S/RES/1368, September 12, 2001.

14. The council's use of this tool has been questioned and criticized by some states as falling outside its mandate. The council, they argue, was not intended to act as a "global legislator." They fear that such action could disrupt the balance of power between the council and the General Assembly as set forth in the UN Charter. Moreover, they assert that having the council, a fifteen-member body not accountable to the other UN organs, impose obligations on all 191 members threatens to weaken one of the cornerstones of traditional international law, namely the principle that international law is based on the consent of states. Others, however, argue that the UN Charter has evolved to allow the council to act as a global legislator under certain circumstances in the face of an urgent security threat; that the "legislation" in question has already won General Assembly approval and a critical mass of state ratifications; and that the council needs to be able to use this tool to address effectively, within the state-centered UN Charter system in which it operates, the threats posed by nonstate terrorists and terrorist groups. For an in-depth discussion of the Security Council's legislative role, see Stefan Talmon, "The Security Council as World Legislature," *American Journal of International Law* 99, no. 1 (January 2005): 175; Eric Rosand, "The Security Council as 'Global Legislator': Ultra Vires or Ultra Innovative," *Fordham International Law Journal* 28 (2005): 542.

15. Kofi Annan, "Statement at Ministerial Level Meeting of the UN Security Council." See United Nations Security Council Resolution 1456, January 20, 2003.

16. Eric Rosand, "Security Council Resolution 1373 and the Counter-Terrorism Committee," in Cyrille Fijnaut, Jan Wouters, and Frederik Naert, eds., *Legal Instruments in the Fight against International Terrorism: A Transatlantic Dialogue* (The Hague: Martinus Nijhoff Publishers, 2004), p. 606.

17. According to the CTC's seventeenth work program, as of September 30, 2005, it had received 613 reports from UN member states. This includes first reports from all 191 States, 169 second reports, 130 third reports, 101 fourth reports, and 22 fifth reports. See Counter-Terrorism Committee, "CTC Programme of Work," http://www.un.org/Docs/sc/committees /1373/programme_of_work.html, accessed December 7, 2005.

18. The Security Council is expected to extend the committee's mandate for an additional two-year period.

19. As of July 2006, the committee has received reports from 129 States, that is, about two-thirds of the UN membership.

20. Christopher Cooper, "Shunned in Sweden: How the Drive to Block Funds for Terrorism Entangled Mr. Aden," *Wall Street Journal,* May 6, 2002.

21. "The 1267 (Al-Qaida/Taliban) Committee and the 1540 (WMD) Sanctions Committee," *Security Council Report,* Update Report no. 5, January 16, 2006.

22. More than forty have still not reported to the committee on steps they are taking to implement the sanctions, as called for by the Security Council in January 2003. For a critical analysis of the work of the Al-Qaida and Taliban Sanctions Committee, see Eric Rosand, "Current Developments: The Security Council's Efforts to Monitor the Implementation of Al-Qaida/Taliban Sanctions," *American Journal of International Law* 98 (2004): 745.

23. As of January 2005, states were reported to have seized or frozen $147 million in assets belonging to 435 individuals and groups linked to al Qaeda or the Taliban. In October 2005 the list included 140 individuals associated with the Taliban and 182 people and 117 businesses or groups linked to al Qaeda. This number is somewhat misleading for a number of reasons. First, between September 11, 2001, and the end of 2001 alone, $112 million in alleged terrorist funds had been frozen (Chantal de Jonge Oudraat, "Combating Terrorism," *The Washington Quarterly* [Autumn 2003]). Second, in the two years after that, only $24 million was frozen. Unspecified "recently published U.S. Treasury report" cited in UN Security Council document S/2003/1070, December 2, 2003, p. 12, footnote c. Little if any of the $24 million was linked to individuals or entities listed on the Al-Qaida and Taliban Sanction Committee's list (UN document S/2003/1070, p. 36). Finally, according to a 2002 independent U.S. expert panel on terrorist finance, "the frequently cited total amount of terrorist-related assets blocked overstates the amount of money taken from al-Qaida and its supporters specifically,

and undoubtedly represents only a small fraction of total funds available to that terrorist organization" (Maurice Greenberg, William F. Wechsler, and Lee S. Wolosky, *Terrorist Financing: Independent Task Force Report* [Washington, D.C.: Brookings Institution, 2002], p. 20).

24. Edward C. Luck, "The Uninvited Challenge: Terrorism Targets the United Nations," Center on International Organization, School of International and Public Affairs, Columbia University, 2005, p. 16, http://www.sipa.columbia.edu/cio/cio/projects/LuckSSRCUNU.pdf, accessed 7 December 2005.

25. See "Delivering Counter-terrorism Assistance," United Nations Office on Drugs and Crime, Terrorism Prevention Branch, April 2005, http://www.unodc.org/pdf/crime/terrorism/Brochure_GPT_April2005.pdf, accessed December 8, 2005).

26. See http://www.unodc.org/unodc/en/money_laundering_technical _assistance.html (accessed June 14, 2006).

27. See "Legal Committee Ends Discussion of Counter-Terrorism Measures; To Receive Group Report on Comprehensive Convention," GA/L/3277, United Nations General Assembly, New York, October 10, 2005, p. 2. During the sixtieth General Assembly, a number of states, including Bahrain, Jordan, Sudan, and the United Arab Emirates, also voiced support for the Saudi Arabian proposal to establish an "anti-terrorism centre" under the auspices of the UN. See UN press releases from Sixth Committee discussions on terrorism, http://www.un.org/News/Press/docs/2005, accessed December 7, 2005. At the October 26, 2005, meeting of the Security Council to discuss the work of its counterterrorism-related committees, Pakistan's permanent representative voiced support for the establishment of an international terrorism centre, along the lines set forth by the Saudi crown prince. See "Statement by Ambassador Munir Akram," http://www.un.int /pakistan/00homesc120605, accessed December 7, 2005.

28. United Nations General Assembly Resolution A/RES/60/43, December 8, 2005.

29. Report of the Secretary-General: "Uniting against Terrorism: Recommendations for a Global Counter-Terrorism Strategy," UN Doc. A/60/825, April 27, 2006.

CHAPTER 3

1. A number of member states, including Costa Rica, Liechtenstein, Pakistan, and Switzerland, have voiced concerns about having the fifteen-member CTC play a coordinating role in the global counterterrorism effort,

believing that neither it nor its parent body is sufficiently representative to play this role effectively over the long run.

2. For a discussion of the Al-Qaida and Taliban Sanctions Committee and 1540 Committee's nascent outreach efforts, see statements by committee chairmen at the October 26, 2005, and May 30, 2006, Security Council meeting to discuss the work of its counterterrorism-related committees. For a summary see "Security Council Briefed by Chairmen of Three Anti-Terrorism Committees; Status of Reporting, Technical Assistance, Among Issues Addressed," SC/8536, United Nations Security Council, New York, October 26, 2005, and "Security Council Reviews Work of Committees on Nuclear Non-Proliferation, Terrorism, Al-Qaida and Taliban," SC/8730, May 30, 2006.

3. See "Statement by the President of the Security Council," S/PRST/2005/16, United Nations Security Council, New York, April 25, 2005; "Statement by the President of the Security Council," S/PRST/2005/34, United Nations Security Council, New York, July 20, 2005; United Nations Security Council Resolution S/RES/1617, July 29, 2005; United Nations Security Council Resolution S/RES/1624, September 14, 2005.

4. See chapter 4 for a discussion of how this formal integration might work.

5. Simon Chesterman, *Shared Secrets: Intelligence and Collective Security* (Sydney, Australia: Lowy Institute for International Policy, 2006), p. 56.

6. For information about the IAEA's budget and staff, see the IAEA's Web site: http://www.iaea.org/About/budget.html and http://www.iaea.org/About/staff.html, accessed December 8, 2005.

7. Of those counterterrorism-related bodies, only the UNODC's TPB and GPML accept voluntary contributions. Voluntary contributions are a major source of funding for most other UN organizations and programs such as the IAEA, UNDP, and the UN Environmental Program.

8. "Questions Relating to the Programme Budget for the Biennium 2004–2005," A/RES/59/276, United Nations General Assembly, New York, January 17, 2005, Section VII, para. 12.

9. The total 2005 budget for the Security Council counterterrorism programs was $12.5 million; for the Al-Qaida and Taliban Monitoring Team, $3,559,300; for the CTED, $6,888,300; and for the 1540 Committee group of experts, $1,794,900. See "Questions Relating to the Programme Budget for the Biennium 2004–2005"; "Estimates in Respect of Special Political Missions, Good Offices and Other Political Initiatives Authorized by the General Assembly and/or the Security Council," A/59/534/Add.1, United Nations General Assembly, New York, November 23, 2004. The TPB's budget for 2005 was $3.5 million, with $1 million coming out of the UN regular budget and the rest coming from voluntary contributions. The GPML's budget for 2005 was approximately $3.2 million in voluntary contributions plus regular budget funding for one post.

10. For a summary of statements at this meeting, see "Security Council Reviews Work of Committees on Nuclear Non-Proliferation, Terrorism, Al-Qaida and Taliban," SC/8730, May 30, 2006.

11. Richard Butler, "Improving Nonproliferation Enforcement," *The Washington Quarterly* (Autumn 2003): 141.

12. Although in Security Council Resolution 1284 (1999) the council established the UN Monitoring Verification Inspection Commission and said that it must approve the appointment of its executive chairman, UNMOVIC was funded out of Iraq oil money and not the regular UN budget.

CHAPTER 4

1. "Mandating and Delivering: Analysis and Recommendations to Facilitate the Review of Mandates," A/60/733, Report of Secretary General of the United Nations, New York, March 30, 2006, paras. 122–23.

2. The Gingrich/Mitchell Task Force on UN Reform highlighted the problem of lack of coordination in the UN counterterrorism program: "Among the solutions that should be explored are mandating closer coordination among the committees (including reducing unnecessary duplication in Member States' reports), combining their staffs, and combining the committees themselves." *American Interests on UN Reform: Report of the Task Force on the United Nations* (Washington, D.C.: United States Institute of Peace, 2005), p. 78. The United States has even suggested that such a consolidation might be necessary. See "Statement by Nicholas Rostow, General Counsel, on the Work of the 1267 Committee, in the Security Council, July 20, 2005," USUN Press Release no. 136 (05), http://www.un.int/usa/05_136.htm, accessed December 8, 2005.

3. See statement by Japan (Kenzo Oshima) at the May 30, 2006, Security Council meeting to discuss the council's counterterrorism program. A summary of the meeting is available online at http://www.un.org/News/Press/docs/2006/sc8730.doc.htm, accessed July 30, 2006.

4. See, for example, the statement by Samoa (Ali'ioaiga Feturi Elisaia) on behalf of Pacific Island Forum at the October 26, 2005, Security Council meeting to discuss the council's counterterrorism program, commenting on the difficulties small states have complying with, implementing, and even understanding the myriad Security Council counterterrorism obligations. Concerns were echoed by Fiji. A summary of the meeting is available online at http://www.un.org/News/Press/docs/2005/sc8536.doc.htm, accessed December 8, 2005. See also statements by Kenya (Wanjuki Muchemi) stating that cooperation among UN divisions and agencies should be strengthened,

and Thailand (Ittiporn Boonpracong), noting that it might be worth exploring the number of UN counterterrorism offices with perhaps overlapping mandates and the establishment of a single UN office such as the High Commissioner on Counter-Terrorism. Both statements available in "Legal Committee, Reviewing Issues on Completion of Overall Anti-Terrorism Treaty, Notes Outstanding Differences," GA/L/3275, United Nations General Assembly, New York, June 10, 2005. See also Suriname (Ewald Lomon), speaking on behalf of the fifteen-member Caribbean Community (CARICOM), who stated that "small countries with limited resources . . . were faced with increasingly onerous responsibilities of meeting obligations established by various United Nations mandates on terrorism." Statement available at "Legal Committee Ends Discussion of Counter-Terrorism Measures; To Receive Group Report on Comprehensive Convention," GA/L/3277, United Nations General Assembly, New York, October 10, 2005, pp. 2–3. Other statements include Syria, which noted the importance of coordination and cooperation among the Security Council committees and their staff bodies, as they will enhance the committees' work and "lighten the burden on countries, especially with regard to the writing of reports, since there is less duplication of information as a result"; and New Zealand, which spoke on behalf of the Pacific Island Forum, and drew attention "to the problems faced by small Member States . . . in meeting the Council's considerable reporting requirements. In the recent Pacific counter-terrorism meeting . . . it was made very clear that the reality of limited resources and the challenge of competing priorities mean that compliance with counter-terrorism remains a significant challenge for many Pacific countries." New Zealand hoped "that the enhanced cooperation among the three committees and expert groups now underway will include some discussion of the consolidation of reporting requirements for small Member States." United Nations Security Council 5229th Meeting, S/PV.5229 (Resumption 1), New York, July 20, 2005, p. 15.

5. By design, the Secretariat currently provides more support to the monitoring team and the 1540 Group of Experts than it provides to the CTED. A consolidation of these two bodies into the larger CTED would reduce Secretariat involvement in the work of those bodies.

6. The TPB has fourteen experts in the field, four of them on full-time assignments and the others working on a part-time basis as local consultants. Jean-Paul Laborde, TPB director, e-mail communication with authors, September 21, 2005.

7. "2005 World Summit Outcome," A/RES/60/1, United Nations General Assembly, New York, October 24, 2005, para. 90.

8. See chapter 3, note 9 for budget figures for UNODC's TPB and GPML.

CHAPTER 5

1. According to one count, there are at least 238 intergovernmental orga-nizations. Michael Barnett and Martha Finnemore, *Rules for the World: International Organizations in Global Politics* (Ithaca, N.Y.: Cornell University Press, 2004), p. 1, citing Union of International Associations, ed., *Yearbook of International Organizations, 2003–2004,* 40th ed., vol. 1B (Munich: K.G. Saur, 2003), p. 2738, app. 3, table 1.

2. See Outcome Document of the March 6, 2003, CTC Conference and United Nations Security Council, Vienna Declaration, S/2004/276, New York, April 1, 2004.

3. Statement by E. Anthony Wayne, Fundacion Jose Ortega y Gasset, November 16, 2005, http://www.state.gov/e/eb/rls/rm/2005/57413.htm, accessed December 9, 2005.

4. Daniel Benjamin, "Work to Institutionalize the International Fight Against Terrorism," in *Restoring American Leadership: Cooperative Steps to Advancing Global Progress* (New York: Open Society Institute and Security and Peace Initiative, 2005), p. 13.

5. A loose analogy could be made to the UN human rights world. There, treaty monitoring bodies such as the Human Rights Committee, which are technical bodies staffed by legal experts from around the world, analyze states' efforts to implement the relevant UN human rights treaty. Although these bodies issue only nonbinding recommendations, because of their tech-nical nature they are often able to be more frank regarding states' imple-mentation efforts than the Human Rights Commission (now Human Rights Council), which is a political body consisting of member states and is thus subject to some of the same limitations that inhibit the UN counter-terror-ism program.

CHAPTER 6

1. Presumably, this could only be done via a decision of the Security Council.

2. The Security Council could continue to manage and update its con-solidated al Qaeda/Taliban list, however, as this is a political activity that properly belongs in the Security Council.

3. Report of the Secretary-General, "Uniting against Terrorism: Recommendations for a Global Counter-Terrorism Strategy," para.70, April 27, 2006, UN Doc. A/60/825.

4. The CTC has the legal authority to do this, but it has not yet acted on it, and is unlikely to do so.

5. In order to have a tie to the new body, the Security Council would likely need, at a minimum, to endorse and agree to accept referrals from the new body. Ideally, the council would go further and formally delegate the current responsibilities of its counterterrorism-related subsidiary bodies to this new organization.

CHAPTER 7

1. For a fuller discussion of the advantages and disadvantages of the different multilateral arrangements, see Francis Fukuyama, *America at the Crossroads: Democracy, Power, and the Neoconservative Legacy* (New Haven, Conn.: Yale University Press, 2006), pp. 155–80, and Shepard Forman and Derk Segaar, "New Coalitions for Global Governance," *Global Governance* (April-June 2006): 205–25.

2. Organizations such as the ICAO, ILO, and WHO are UN specialized agencies, established pursuant to Article 57 of the UN Charter, reporting to the fifty-three-member ECOSOC. The IAEA is not a specialized agency, but an independent international organization under the aegis of the UN. Organizations such as the IOM and OPCW are outside the UN family, although the latter does report to the General Assembly. Neither the council, the General Assembly, or ECOSOC set the policy of any of these bodies. In all instances, the policy is set by the member state governing body established by the founding document.

3. The Wassenaar Arrangement, for example, was established in June 1995 with a declaration issued in The Hague signed by seventeen states. A number of the other multilateral export control regimes (for example, the Nuclear Suppliers Group and the Australia Group) do not have a formal constitutive document beyond their respective agreed guidelines and control lists. See the Nuclear Suppliers Group's Guidelines for Nuclear Transfers and Guidelines for Transfers of Nuclear-Related Dual-Use Equipment, Materials, Software and Related Technology, both available in "Communications Received from Certain Member States Regarding Guidelines for the Export of Nuclear Material, Equipment and Technology," INFCIRC/254/Rev.7/Part 1, International Atomic Energy Agency, Vienna, February 23, 2005; and "Communications Received from Certain Member States Regarding Guidelines for Transfers of Nuclear-related Dual-use Equipment, Materials, Software and Related Technology," INFCIRC/254/Rev.6/Part 2, International Atomic Energy Agency, Vienna, February 23, 2005.

4. Information about the membership of these bodies is available on their respective Web sites. See "Financial Action Task Force," http://www.fatf-gafi.org; "Wassenaar Arrangement," http://www.wassenaar.org; "International Atomic Energy Agency," http://www.iaea.org; "Missile Technology Control Regime," http://www.mtcr.info; "Egmont Group," http://www.egmontgroup.org.

5. For example, the MTCR takes decisions to admit a new partner by consensus. In making membership decisions, members "tend to consider whether a prospective new Member would strengthen international non-proliferation efforts, demonstrates a sustained and sustainable commitment to non-proliferation, has a legally based effective export control system that puts into effect the MTCR Guidelines and procedures, and administers and enforces such controls effectively. The regime's dialogue with prospective partners is conducted through the MTCR Chair, visits to capitals by teams comprised of representatives of four MTCR partners and bilateral exchanges." See "MTCR Partners," Missile Technology Control Regime, http://www.mtcr.info/english/partners.html, accessed December 9, 2005.

6. A notable exception is the FATF, which has a small (ten-person, including support staff) technical secretariat working out of, but independent from, the Organisation for Economic Co-operation and Development in Paris. This secretariat works together with FATF members in carrying out the mutual evaluations that form a core part of FATF's work. The Wassenaar Arrangement also has a small secretariat of seven experts and five support staff, all of whom are attached to the UN office in Vienna.

7. See, for example, the 1994 Chemical Weapons Convention establishing the OPCW, the 1958 International Maritime Organization Convention establishing the IMO, and the 1944 Chicago Convention establishing the ICAO.

8. Although there is no legal barrier to the Security Council doing so, it does not appear that the council has formally delegated any of its authorities to a non–Security Council, let alone non-UN, body. The closest, albeit imperfect, analogy would be in the area of international humanitarian law, with the establishment of the International Criminal Court (ICC). The court, in the mind of some council members, would obviate the need to create any more ad hoc criminal tribunals. The work of the existing council-established ad hoc tribunals, however, was not affected by the creation of the ICC. Although all UN members do not support the ICC as it stands, there was broad support for the need to establish a permanent international criminal court.

9. For example, the Convention on the Prohibition of the Development, Production, Stockpiling and Use of Chemical Weapons and on their Destruction ("Chemical Weapons Convention"), which established the

OPCW, took nearly twenty years to negotiate within the Conference on Disarmament in Geneva and another four years to acquire the necessary ratifications to enter into force. The statute of the IAEA was approved after some three years of negotiation and came into force the following year. The treaty that led to the establishment of the World Customs Organization took some six years to finalize and a seventh year to enter into force.

10. The G20 is an informal forum of both G8 countries and countries from the global South, established in 1999. It seeks to promote an open and constructive dialogue between industrial nations and emerging-market countries on key issues relating to the international monetary and financial system and, in the process, to help strengthen the international financial architecture. In addition, it provides its members, from a range of major countries at varying stages of development, with a platform for discussing current international economic questions.

11. The UNDP began operations in 1966 as a result of General Assembly Resolution 2029 (XX) (1965), which combined the UN Expanded Programme of Technical Assistance with the Special Fund. General Assembly Resolution 2688 (XXV) (1970) took effect in 1971 and defined the organizational structure and activities of UNDP. General Assembly Resolution 57 (I) (1946) established the UN International Children's Emergency Fund (UNICEF) to provide emergency assistance to children in war-ravaged countries following World War II. General Assembly Resolution 802 (VII) (1953) placed the fund on a permanent footing and charged it with addressing the long-term needs of children and mothers in developing countries, changing its name to the UN Children's Fund, while retaining the UNICEF acronym. The UN Environment Programme (UNEP) was established by General Assembly Resolution 2997 (XXVII) (1972) following the Stockholm Conference on Human Environment.

12. Although most treaty-based organizations that are part of the UN family use the UN scale of assessments, under which the United States pays some 22 percent of the organization's regular budget, some use a different one. ICAO assessments, for example, are based on a country's economic factors and relative importance in civil aviation, as measured by passenger/freight mileage flown, with a maximum assessment of 25 percent. Assessments to the International Maritime Organization are based chiefly on registered shipping tonnage, with major open-registry countries (those that register ships but do not necessarily own them, for example Cyprus, Liberia, Panama, and the Bahamas) paying large assessments. See "United States Participation in the United Nations, 2004," pp. 86, 96, http://www.state.gov/p/io/conrpt/partic, accessed April 15, 2006.

13. A small percentage of the budgets of UN programs such as UNEP and UNDP come from the UN regular budget, with the rest coming from voluntary contributions.

14. Many of the existing treaty-based organizations have a thirty- to forty-member state executive council or governing board that meets a handful of times a year to take the necessary policy decisions that enable the technical secretariat to function. For example, the forty-one-member executive council of the OPCW meets four to five times per year, and more frequently in meetings and informal consultations to take policy decisions. The thirty-six-member ICAO council is chosen by the more broadly representative assembly, which includes all 189 member states.

15. For example, the thirty-six-member ICAO council "consists of States of chief importance in air transport, States which make the largest contribution to the provision of facilities for air navigation, and States whose designation will ensure that all major areas of the world are represented." See the International Civil Aviation Organization, http://www.icao.org /icao/en/howworks.htm, accessed December 9, 2005. In addition, of the thirty-five seats on the IAEA board of governors, ten are reserved for states "most advanced in the technology of atomic energy including the production of source materials," including one in each of eight geographical areas. See the International Atomic Energy Agency, http://www.iaea.org/About /statute.html, accessed December 9, 2005. Most recently, the newly established Peacebuilding Commission reserves seats on its Organizational Committee for the top five contributors to various UN program budgets and the top five providers of military personnel and civilian police to UN missions. General Assembly Resolution, A/60/180, December 30, 2005.

16. Like the World Bank, the IMF governing structure is designed to reflect the preferences of the IMF's richest and most powerful members. Unlike many international organizations established in the past fifty years, the IMF weighs the voting power of its 184 members according to their contributions to its resources. The more money a country contributes to the IMF, the more votes it receives. Individual states, however, cannot increase their voting power by simply giving more money. Rather, the IMF's executive board decides how much states will be allowed to contribute. As a result of this arrangement, the United States, Japan, Germany, France, and the United Kingdom control more than 40 percent of the voting power in the IMF. Barnett and Finnemore, *Rules for the World*, p. 49. Professor Fukuyama suggests that it would be reasonable to change NATO's consensus-based decision-making process, for example, to one that was based on weighted votes. Fukuyama, *America at the Crossroads*, 174.

17. The FATF, for example, has granted observer status to more than twenty international and regional organizations. In addition, the UNDP established a Bureau for Resources and Strategic Partnerships "to coordinate and nurture its working relationships with donor countries, civil society organizations, international financial institutions, regional development banks, the private sector and rest of the UN system." See "Strategic

Partnerships," United Nations Development Programme, http://www. undp.org/partnerships, accessed December 9, 2005.

18. For example, on the UNDP thirty-six-member executive board, eight seats are reserved for the African Group, seven for the Asian and Pacific Group, four for the Eastern European Group, five for the Latin American and Caribbean Group, and twelve for the Western European and Other Group. In addition, the fifty-nine-member UNEP governing council reserves sixteen seats for African Group states, ten for Latin American Group states, thirteen for Asian states, fourteen for Western European and Other Group states, and six for Eastern European states. See "Member States of the Governing Council of the United Nations Environmental Programme for the Period 2004–2007," United Nations Environmental Programme, http://www.unep.org/gc/GCSS-VIII/memberstates-geographic.pdf, accessed December 9, 2004.

19. While the rules of procedure of some of the UN program governing boards allow for voting, this option is rarely utilized, with most boards seeking to take decisions by consensus. The UNDP executive board's rules of procedure, for example, provide that the "practice of striving for consensus in decision-making shall be encouraged." "Rules of Procedure of the Executive Board of the United Nations Development Programme and of the United Nations Population Fund," DP/1997/32, United Nations Development Programme, New York, May 1997.

20. Portions of the MCTR were expanded in January 2003 to deter terrorists from acquiring missiles and missile technology. "Plenary Meeting of the Missile Technology Control Regime," Missile Technology Control Regime, September 19–26, 2003, http://www.mtcr.info/english/press/buenosaires.html, accessed December 9, 2005. The regime was also bolstered in November 2002, when members created a new voluntary initiative called the International Code of Conduct Against Ballistic Missile Proliferation. Steven A. Mirmina, "Reducing the Proliferation of Orbital Debris: Alternatives to a Legally Binding Instrument," *American Journal of International Law* 99 (2005): 649, 655. The FATF expanded its mandate in fall 2001 to include the fight against terrorist financing and the introduction of eight special recommendations (now nine) in this area. "FATF Mandate Renewed for Eight Years," Financial Action Task Force, May 14, 2004, http://www.fatf-gafi.org/dataoecd/46/33/35065565.pdf, accessed December 9, 2005.

21. The FATF, for example, periodically reviews its mission and extends its mandate. Its current mandate runs from 2004 to 2012, at which time it will need to take a decision on whether to renew the mandate or dissolve the body. "FATF Mandate Renewed for Eight Years," Financial Action Task Force, May 14, 2004, http://www.fatf-gafi.org/dataoecd/46/33/35065565.pdf, accessed December 9, 2005.

22. UNAIDS's mandate is to provide leadership and advocacy for effective action against the epidemic; strategic information and technical support to guide efforts against AIDS worldwide; tracking, monitoring, and evaluation of the epidemic and responses to it; civil society engagement and the development of strategic partnerships; and mobilization of resources to support an effective response. See United Nations Programme on HIV/AIDS, http://www.unaids.org, accessed December 9, 2005.

23. See The Global Fund, http://theglobalfund.org, accessed December 9, 2005. The Global Fund has raised nearly $5 billion in less than four years. See http://www.theglobalfund.org/en/files/pledges&contributions.xls, accessed April 15, 2006.

CHAPTER 8

1. U.S. President George W. Bush has remarked, "The global threat of terrorism requires a global response." White House, "President Bush Discusses Progress in the War on Terror."

2. *9/11 Commission Report*, p. xiv.

3. See statement by Frances Fragos Townsend, "Keynote Address (as delivered) by Frances Fragos Townsend," United States Institute of Peace, Washington, D.C., September 19, 2005, http://www.usip.org/events/2005/townsend.pdf, accessed December 9, 2005.

4. Statement of Donald H. Rumsfeld, Senate Appropriations Committee, FY 2006 Supplemental Request, March 9, 2006, http://appropriations.senate.gov/hearmarkups/Secdef_SAC_statement_for_submission2.pdf.

5. Statement by Juan C. Zarate, House International Relations Subcommittee on the Middle East and Central Asia, March 24, 2004, http://www.treas.gov/press/releases/js1257.htm, accessed December 9, 2005.

6. Maurice R. Greenberg et al., "Update on the Global Campaign Against Terrorist Financing," Second Report of an Independent Task Force on Terrorist Financing, Council on Foreign Relations, New York, June 15, 2004, http://www.cfr.org/content/publications/attachments/Revised_Terrorist_Financing.pdf, accessed December 9, 2005.

7. According to the *9/11 Commission Report*, U.S. and foreign intelligence officials list six regions as being the most likely ones in which terrorist leaders would relocate their bases: western Pakistan and the Pakistan/Afghanistan border, southern/western Afghanistan, the Arabian peninsula, southeast Asia (from Thailand to the southern Philippines to Indonesia), West Africa (including Niger and Mali), and "European cities

with expatriate Muslim communities, especially central and eastern European cities where security forces and border controls are less effective." *9/11 Commission Report*, p. 366.

8. See, for example, Benjamin and Simon, *The Next Attack*, p. 204.

9. Ibid.; Michael B. Kraft, "Congressional Conferees Cut Counterterrorism Programs," *The Counterterrorism Blog*, November 3, 2005, http://counterterror.typepad.com/the_counterterrrorism_ blog/2005/11/congressional_c.html, accessed December 9, 2005.

10. For more information about this State Department program, see "Antiterrorism Assistance Program," U.S. Department of State, http://www.state.gov/m/ds/terrorism/c8583.htm, accessed December 9, 2005.

11. *9/11 Commission Report*, p. 366.

12. Statement by E. Anthony Wayne.

13. Ibid.

14. Scott Shane, "Intelligence Center Is Created for Unclassified Information," *New York Times*, November 9, 2005.

15. Ibid.

16. Chesterman, *Shared Secrets*, p. 64.

17. "The Department of Homeland Security: Information Analysis and Infrastructure Protection," The White House, http://www.whitehouse.gov /deptofhomeland/sect6.html, accessed December 12, 2005.

18. Ibid.

19. See "Transnational Threats Update 3," no. 11, Center for Strategic and International Studies, October 2005, p. 7, http://www.csis.org /component/option,com_csis_pubs/task,view/id,2107/, accessed December 12, 2005.

20. Ibid.

21. See "America's Place in the World 2005: Opinion Leaders Turn Cautious, Public Looks Homeward," Pew Research Center for the People & the Press and Council on Foreign Relations, November 17, 2005, p. 1, http://www.cfr.org/publication/9225, accessed December 12, 2005.

22. See ibid., pp. 27–28.

23. Luck, "The Uninvited Challenge," p. 22.

24. See, for example, Jeffrey Laurenti, "Global Goals, Modest Results: The UN in Search of Reform," *Current History* (December 2005): 432.

25. G8 Statement on Strengthening the UN's Counter-Terrorism Program, St. Petersburg, Russia, July 16, 2006, available at http://en.g8russia.ru /docs/18.html, accessed July 31, 2006.

26. "Declaration on Combating Terrorism Is Adopted in Brussels," Council of the European Union, 2004, http://www.eu2004.ie/templates /news.asp?sNavlocator=66&list_id=462.

CHAPTER 9

1. Daniel Benjamin, "Work to Institutionalize the International Fight Against Terrorism," p. 4.

2. Author interview with Kenyan officials, Nairobi, March 13–19, 2006. See also Volker Krause and Eric E. Otenyo, "Terrorism and the Kenyan Public," *Studies in Conflict and Terrorism* 28, no. 2 (March–April 2005): 99–112.

3. Jeffrey Herbst and Greg Mills, "Africa and the War on Terror," *South African Journal of International Affairs* 10 (Winter/Spring 2002). The G77 is the largest third world coalition in the United Nations. It provides developing world countries a means for articulating and promoting collective interests in the UN, often via the presentation of a common position. Given that there are now 132 countries in the G77, this group wields significant power in the 191-member General Assembly. See http://www.g77.org/main/gen_info_1.htm (accessed June 14, 2006).

4. "Human Security in East Asia International Conference on Human Security in East Asia," Korean National Commission for UNESCO, Seoul, Korea, June 16–17, 2003.

5. Bruno Stagno, Statement to United Nations General Assembly, Third Committee, New York, October 8, 2004, http://un.cti.depaul.edu, accessed December 12, 2005.

6. United Nations General Assembly Resolution A/RES/60/43, December 8, 2005.

7. Interview with Bruno Stagno, Costa Rica Ambassador to the UN, December 13, 2005.

8. See *Final Report of the Counter-Terrorism International Conference,* Counter-Terrorism International Conference, Riyadh, February 5–8, 2005, http://www.ctic.org.sa, accessed December 12, 2005.

9. "Final Communiqué of the Annual Coordination Meeting of Ministers for Foreign Affairs of the States Members of the Organization of the Islamic Conference," A/60/440, S/2005/658, United Nations General Assembly Security Council, New York, October 19, 2005, para. 60.

10. Mazen Mahdi, "GCC States Likely to Adopt Saudi Proposal for Combating Terror," *Arab News,* November 27, 2005.

11. See Statement by Ambassador Munir Akram, June 14, 2006, text available at http://www.un.int/pakistan/00home52206, accessed July 31, 2006.

12. See ibid.

13. Letter from Egyptian Foreign Minister Ahmed Aboul Gheit to UN Secretary-General Kofi Annan, September 1, 2005, UN document A/60/359.

14. Annex to the Letter dated September 30, 2005, from the Permanent Representative of Egypt to the United Nations addressed to the Chairman of the Sixth Committee, UN document A/C.6/60/2.

15. See, for example, *Helping Prevent Violent Conflict*, DAC Guidelines, Organisation for Economic Co-operation and Development, 2001, p. 37, http://www.oecd.org/dataoecd/15/54/1886146.pdf, accessed June 4, 2006.

16. For example, in July 2003 the Japanese government "released a new draft ODA charter, which refers to promoting Japan's own security and to combating terrorism. A new focus on activities relating to security system reform may herald a shift away from the traditional Japanese emphasis on big infrastructure projects. Japanese ODA to the Philippines exemplifies this shift." See "Conflict Security, and Official Development Assistance (ODA): Issues for NGO Advocacy," Global Security and Development Network, http://www.bond.org.uk/pubs/advocacy/gsdpaper.pdf, accessed December 12, 2005.

INDEX

Tables and notes are indicated by "*t*" and "*n*."

ABOUT THE AUTHORS

ALISTAIR MILLAR is the director of the Center on Global Counter-Terrorism Cooperation, a nonpartisan research and policy institute that works to improve internationally coordinated responses to the continually evolving threat of terrorism by providing governments and international organizations with timely, policy-relevant research, analysis, and recommendations. He also teaches at the Elliott School of International Affairs at The George Washington University in Washington, D.C. Previously, he was a senior analyst at the British American Security Information Council (BASIC), where he focused on NATO and European security issues. He has served as a consultant to U.S. foundations and foreign governments on nuclear proliferation and counterterrorism issues. He has written numerous chapters, articles, and reports on international counterterrorism efforts, sanctions regimes, and nonproliferation and is editor of *Tactical Nuclear Weapons: Emergent Threats in an Evolving Security Environment* (Brassey's, 2003). His opinion editorials and articles have appeared in publications and periodicals including the *Los Angeles Times, Defense News,* and the *Journal of International Affairs.*

ERIC ROSAND is a senior fellow at the Center on Global Counter-Terrorism Cooperation. He served in the U.S. Department of State for nearly nine years. Most recently, he was chief of the Multilateral Affairs Unit in the Department of State's Office of the Counter-terrorism Coordinator, where he was responsible for developing and coordinating the United States government's counterterrorism policies at the UN and other multilateral institutions. From 2002 to 2005, he was the deputy legal counselor at the U.S. Mission to the UN, where he served as the mission's counterterrorism expert and representative to the Security Council's Counter-Terrorism Committee and General Assembly's Ad Hoc Committee on Terrorism. He has been intimately involved in nearly all of the major counterterrorism developments at the UN since September 11, 2001. Prior to that he served as a lawyer at the Department of State, where he worked on rule of law issues in Bosnia and Holocaust-era compensation and restitution issues. He is the author of numerous articles and book chapters on the appropriate role for the UN in the counterterrorism campaign.